THE
SAND HOUSE

Above: Sand House front garden, looking north.

Below: Long Room interior *c.* 1912.

— THE —
SAND HOUSE

A Victorian Marvel
Revisited

Richard Bell & Peter Tuffrey

AMBERLEY

The Cloisters facing south.

This book is dedicated to William and Henry Senior

First published 1988

Amberley Publishing
Cirencester Road, Chalford,
Stroud, Gloucestershire, GL6 8PE

www.amberleybooks.com

British Library Cataloguing in Publication Data.
A catalogue record for this book is available from the British Library.

ISBN 978-1-4456-0117-5

Typesetting and Origination by Amberley Publishing.
Printed in Great Britain.

Contents

	Acknowledgements	6
	Introduction	7
Chapter 1	William Senior and the Sand Pit	9
Chapter 2	Henry Senior and the Sand House	23
Chapter 3	The Tunnels and Carvings	47
Chapter 4	The Sand House in Corporation Ownership	65
Chapter 5	The Hemingways and No. 69 Victoria Street	79
Chapter 6	Echoes from the Past	91
Epilogue	And Finally... Or Perhaps Not?	117
	Figures and References	121

Note

For simplicity the Sand House 'complex' will be referred to throughout this book as the Sand House, unless the tunnels themselves are specifically mentioned. It should be noted at this point that the house has been known at various times as Senior's Rock House and Don Castle. However, Sand House is the term which has been used almost exclusively since the early twentieth century and this, therefore, is the name which will be adopted henceforth.

Acknowledgements

The authors wish to express their gratitude to the following people, some of whom have passed away since research began on the previous version of the book in the mid-1980s:

Winifred Brackenbury, Eric Braim, David Brewster, Paul Buckland, Harry Claxton, John Cuttriss, Malcolm Deakin, Harold Dean, Edwin Dixon, Nancy Dobson, Malcolm Dolby, Alan Drinkall, Maurice Dunston, Kenneth Elliff, Doris L. Firth, David Fordham, Tom Fox, Terry Friedman, Thomas Hague, Graham Harris, Ken Haywood, Cyril Hemingway, Charles Hippisley-Fox, Marie Hutchinson, David John, Mike Kallaur, Dr Charles Kelham and Staff at Doncaster Archives and Local Studies Library, Martin Limbert, John Little, Ada Lumby, Annie Lumby, David Mahoney, Anne Mallender, Doris Mason, George Merrills, Graham Middleton, Reg. Middleton, Chris Palmer, Anne Pennington-George, Derek Porter, Anne Proctor, Steve Rimmington, Brian Senior, John Senior, Lawrence Senior, Olive Senior, Matthew Shelton, Walter Shikell, Brian Skidmore, Graham and Irene Slack, Syd Slack, Joan Smith, John Smith, Pat Smith, Edna Straw, Susan Street, Bob Taylor, Andrew Timms, Martin Timms, Tristram Tuffrey, Mrs J. Warnock, Philip Weston, West Yorkshire County Record Office Staff, Paul Wheeldon, Edna Wilson and Sandra Winter.

Front garden in snow.

Introduction

In the early 1960s, when I was about nine or ten, I learned that my family was associated with Doncaster's famous Sand House, which had formerly been one of the town's most noted landmarks. At family gatherings my relatives talked about the house and its associated tunnels and they showed their cherished photographs of the area, handed down from earlier generations. However, it was not until the early 1980s that I seriously became interested in discovering more information about both the Sand House and the two men responsible for its inception, my maternal great-great-great-grandfather William Senior, and his son Henry. A colleague, gathering information about his own family history, had prompted me to look into the past and discover more information about my own ancestors. Consequently, I began the task of making a family tree and collecting newspaper articles and other memorabilia. I soon began concentrating on tracing my mother's antecedents, since these were the people who were connected with the Sand House. As might have been expected, my maternal grandmother proved to be one of my early sources of information. She provided me with essential background details about the Sand House, its legends and its main characters.

My enthusiasm for the project was greatly enhanced in 1984 when I was given the opportunity, by the Doncaster Metropolitan Borough Council's Engineering Division, to inspect some of the remaining Sand House tunnels. This was shortly before they were filled in and the few remaining traces of the Sand House were obliterated. After inspecting the tunnels, I experienced both anger and sorrow. I felt anger because I considered that from 1900, when the Sand House was purchased by Doncaster Corporation, the area had been systematically destroyed. I felt sorrow because this unique feature, which could have been a tremendous tourist attraction for the town, would never be seen by future generations.

Soon after my visit to the tunnels I met Peter Tuffrey, a well-known local historian and author of many books on the Doncaster area, who also had a keen interest in the Sand House. We agreed that our combined skills and knowledge made us well-suited to producing a book together. So, as a book was the only way in which the Sand House's existence could be recorded for posterity and appreciated both now and in the future, we continued our research with this ultimate aim in mind.

By reading numerous articles and studying maps and reports on the Sand House, it became quite clear to us that the area's history was in a muddle. Newspapers contained many inaccuracies and often perpetuated myths and fallacies. An example of this occurred during the 1960s when, in an article, Henry Senior was wrongly referred to as George Senior. In subsequent years the press continually recorded that George Senior (who was, in fact, Henry's son) was the person responsible for the Sand House and its tunnels. Also, the articles never mentioned that the Sand House really came into being as an indirect result of excavating a tunnel through William Senior's land to accommodate a sewer.

The first book which Peter and I produced, entitled *The Sand House – A Victorian Marvel*, was published in 1988 and all copies sold out some years ago. However, from my many illustrated talks on the subject and the generally increased level of interest in local history, it became clear that a second book was called for.

For the current project we decided not merely to reproduce that which had appeared in 1988, but to create a more comprehensive work. We have used both additional material that has been obtained in the intervening years and items omitted from the first book, which modern technology now enables us to present to the appropriate quality standard. The original principle of the first book still applies, in that we have attempted to present the reader with a true chronology of the Sand House's history and to describe its association with the Senior family.

There are still some aspects of which Peter and I are uncertain and we have drawn attention to these in the text. For example, very little has been discovered about the Senior family's business dealings, despite this being an integral part of the Sand House development. Also, our lack of certainty as to which photographs, if any, show Henry Senior himself, is a continuing source of frustration. These and other aspects provide further avenues of research for us and possibly any suitably inspired reader. Hopefully, no new myths or fallacies will be created in the current piece of work.

Being a member of a family associated with the Sand House has had its advantages. Various photographs and items of information have been handed down through generations, and I am grateful to all my relatives who have helped with the project. However, having close Sand House connections has also had disadvantages, because on some occasions my urge to discover every minute detail about the subject has led me to wander from the main theme. For this reason I am grateful to Peter, who has kept us focussed on the core objectives.

Finally, I should like to reiterate that if the Sand House were still intact today it would surely have become a splendid tourist attraction. I hope this book will serve as a fitting tribute to a once renowned and truly unique element of the Doncaster townscape, which has now sadly disappeared.

Richard Bell, 2010.

Chapter One

William Senior
and the Sand Pit

Fig. 1.1 The Great Fungus in the 'sewerage tunnel.'

WILLIAM SENIOR AND THE SAND PIT

The Sand House story's first major character is William Senior. He was born, a groom's son, at Tanshelf near Pontefract, during 1802. Unfortunately, little is known about his early life or when and why he moved to Doncaster. The first located reference to his presence in the town was in 1825 when his first child, Henry, was baptised there. William's occupation is not mentioned in the relevant baptism record, but by 1831 he is noted in a deed as being a gardener and seedsman. The deed also notes that he owned, along with his hairdresser brother Edwin, land in Duke Street. William's workplace in 1831 is unclear, but it is thought to have been Balby Lane Close, on Doncaster's south-western outskirts, since he purchased this land from the trustees of the late Richard Maw, in May 1832. The area of the property was slightly less than two acres. As well as containing a market garden, a pump and several cottages (one of which was built by William Senior), it also included a small sand pit. Although this feature, in the early 1830s, was no more than 30 m (100 feet) long by 12 m (40 feet) wide, it nevertheless established an important connection between sand and the Senior family. Balby Lane Close was situated alongside Burden Lane (formerly Thief Lane), a narrow road connecting St Sepulchre Gate (the main thoroughfare leading south-westwards out of Doncaster) and Green Dyke Lane. Its location can be seen in Fig. 1.2.

In the early part of the nineteenth century, Doncaster was described as being 'pleasantly situated on the south bank of the River Don and one of the most clean, airy and elegant towns in the British Dominion' (Baines, 1822). The Great North Road from London to Edinburgh passed through the centre of the town, taking in its range Hall Gate, High Street and French Gate. Local tradespeople derived considerable benefits from the incessant traffic along the road. However, there was not much general trade in the town, several attempts to establish manufacturing industries having failed earlier. Baines' 1822 directory does not record any sand merchants resident in Doncaster and it is probable that when William began his sand business ten years later, he was one of the first people to hold this occupation. The sand was used in the building trade and in various foundries, since it was valuable in making moulds for castings. A geological overview was given in 1987 by Mrs Anne

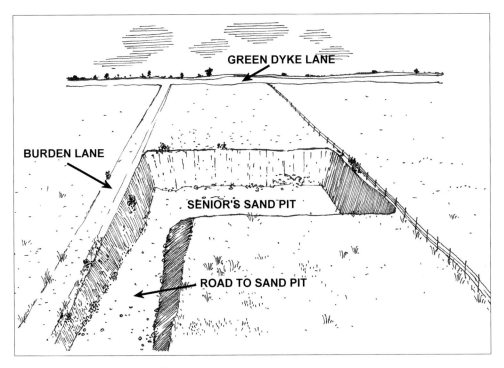

GREEN DYKE LANE

BURDEN LANE

SENIOR'S SAND PIT

ROAD TO SAND PIT

Fig. 1.2 Artist's impression of Senior's sand pit *c.* 1830s.

Pennington-George, Doncaster Museum & Art Gallery's Education and Geology officer:

The [sand] was excavated in sedimentary rocks called the Sherwood Sandstones Group (formerly known as the Bunter Sandstone). Their soft, friable nature made it suitable for easy digging.

The Sherwood Sandstones belong to the geological period called the Trias which started millions of years ago. During that time Britain lay just north of the Equator within the vast supercontinent called PANGAEA, which later split into the present day continents. The Doncaster area was a barren, semi-arid desert, and the Sherwood Sandstone was deposited in shallow water (evidence being seen in the current bedding and ripple marks of the sandstone). Its brick-red colour is due to staining with ferric oxide and its permeable nature means that it is a valuable AQUIFER (water-bearing rock) supplying Doncaster with an underground water supply.

When Edwin White's trade directory was published in 1837, it was the first time that any Seniors were noted as Doncaster tradespeople. In the directory, William Senior was recorded as a sand merchant in 'Sand Pit Quay' (or 'Key'), the name adopted for the northern part of Balby Lane Close, adjacent to St Sepulchre Gate. The origin of the name 'Sand Pit Quay' is unknown, but almost certainly had some connection with 'Sand Pit Lock,' a parcel of William Senior's land situated approximately half a mile away, in Balby.

The 1841 Census notes William Senior as a gardener with a wife and five children. Three years later the dangers of quarrying were amply demonstrated when a fateful accident occurred in William's sand pit. Details were given in the *Doncaster, Nottingham and Lincoln Gazette* of 8 November 1844:

> Dreadful Death – An inquest was held at the Mansion-House, in this town, on Saturday last, before Mr. Mandall, coroner, and a respectable jury, on view of the body of Robert Hall, twenty-eight years of age, of Epworth who was unfortunately killed in the Sand Pit of Mr. Senior, on the line of the Balby Road, near the Shakespeare's Head, on the preceding day. The deceased was employed in clearing away the sand preparatory to blasting the main body of the stratum. Some danger of the upper portion giving way was indicated. An alarm was given; but the deceased, who was unhappily deaf, did not hear the summons; nor was there immediately afterwards time to do so more effectually. The mass of sand fell upon him, and, in consequence of the position in which he was placed, with the spade in his hand, his heart and entrails were forced out, and he was, of course, killed instantaneously. He had no family; and had only been employed in the pit a short period. Mr. Senior's son [Henry] and a man of the name of Hall fortunately escaped. A cart which was standing near the spot was broken to pieces. The jury returned a verdict of "accidental death."

Henry was William's eldest son and, later in this book, will become the Sand House's second major character. He was married in Doncaster, at the age of nineteen or twenty, to Mary Gray, and shortly afterwards moved to a location near the Dearne and Dove Canal at Barnsley, becoming a book-keeper and lock-keeper. It is thought that he resided at Junction Lock, where the Barnsley Canal joined the Dearne and Dove Canal, but surprisingly, reference to this dwelling was omitted from the 1851 Census. Although Henry leaves the story at this stage, his involvement with the Sand House will be dealt with in subsequent chapters.

A plan illustrating the land ownership in the Balby Lane Close area, between *c.* 1820 and *c.* 1870, may be seen in Fig. 1.3.

In Doncaster around the mid-nineteenth century, several major events occurred which changed the whole character of the town. They can also be considered as landmarks in the Sand House's development. During 1848 the Great Northern Railway Company extended its line from London to York, becoming established through Doncaster. This development ensured Doncaster's continued importance in the country's communications network. Furthermore, the railway line's convenience and importance was immeasurable, both to the travelling public and to merchants and manufacturers. Four years later Doncaster's Local Board of Health (established 1851) decided that, because the town had witnessed a marked expansion since the advent of the railways, a system of main drains, or sewers, needed to be constructed. The proposed route of one of these drains extended from Hall Gate along Horse Fair (Waterdale), St James' Street, and then through William Senior's land to an outfall beyond Green Dyke Lane, on the Carr (Fig. 1.4). Contractors David White, John Meggitt and John Marshall began work on the project during 1853 and the *D. N. L. Gaz.* of 13 May 1853, under the heading 'Doncaster Board of Health,' gave an account of events:

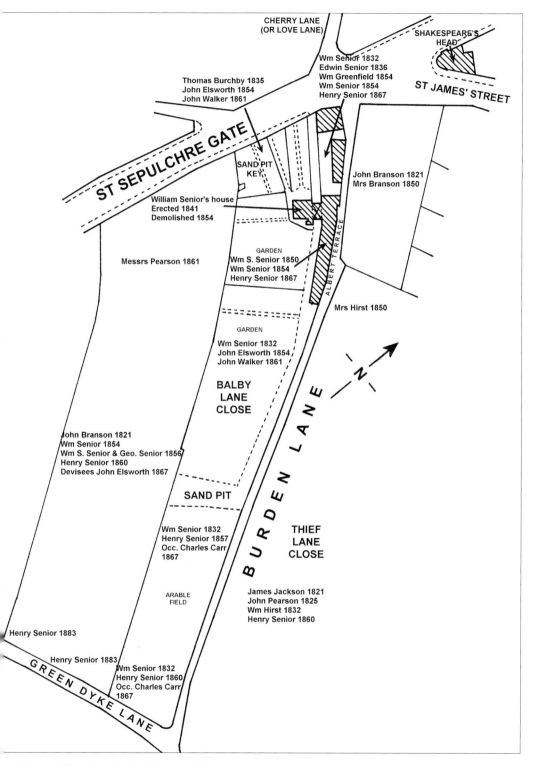

CHERRY LANE
(OR LOVE LANE)

SHAKESPEARE'S
HEAD

Wm Senior 1832
Edwin Senior 1836
Wm Greenfield 1854
Wm Senior 1854
Henry Senior 1867

ST JAMES' STREET

Thomas Burchby 1835
John Elsworth 1854
John Walker 1861

ST SEPULCHRE GATE

SAND PIT
KEY

John Branson 1821
Mrs Branson 1850

William Senior's house
Erected 1841
Demolished 1854

GARDEN
Wm S. Senior 1850
Wm Senior 1854
Henry Senior 1867

ALBERT TERRACE

Messrs Pearson 1861

Mrs Hirst 1850

GARDEN

Wm Senior 1832
John Elsworth 1854
John Walker 1861

BALBY
LANE
CLOSE

BURDEN LANE

N

John Branson 1821
Wm Senior 1854
Wm S. Senior & Geo. Senior 1856
Henry Senior 1860
Devisees John Elsworth 1867

SAND PIT

Wm Senior 1832
Henry Senior 1857
Occ. Charles Carr
1867

THIEF
LANE
CLOSE

ARABLE
FIELD

James Jackson 1821
John Pearson 1825
Wm Hirst 1832
Henry Senior 1860

Henry Senior 1883

Henry Senior 1883

GREEN DYKE LANE

Wm Senior 1832
Henry Senior 1860
Occ. Charles Carr
1867

Fig. 1.3 Plan showing land ownership *c.* 1820 – *c.* 1870.

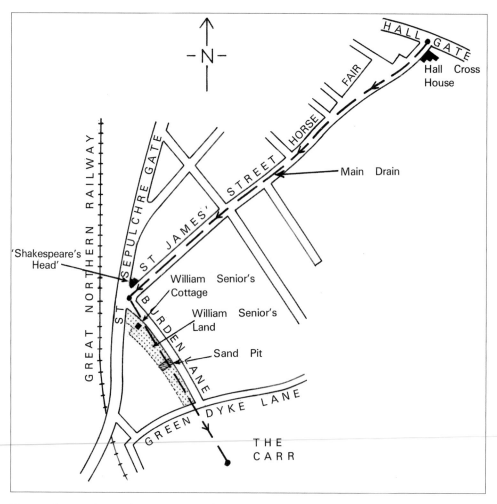

Fig. 1.4 Route of main drain constructed *c.* 1854.

A meeting of the Local Board of Health of the Borough of Doncaster, was held in the Council Chamber of the Guild-Hall, on Wednesday morning last ... The Clerk read a recommendation from the board that £50 be allowed to Mr [William] Senior for permitting the making of a drain required to pass through his land, and also for allowing any authorised agent of the board to make such repairs at the drain as might in future be required. The draft of an agreement to the above effect was prepared, sealed and accepted, and the board acceded to the sum proposed.

The land along the drain's route rose in elevation from the Shakespeare's Head public house in St Sepulchre Gate to a high point in Green Dyke Lane, falling away again as it approached the Carr. Consequently, to minimise the depth of excavation, a tunnel was made through the high ground to allow the drain to slope down from St Sepulchre Gate until it reached its outfall. The tunnel began in William's sand pit and achieved a maximum depth of 13 m (43 feet) below Green Dyke Lane. The length of drain from St Sepulchre Gate to the sand pit was constructed in a trench, while through the tunnel it was located beneath the floor (Figs 1.5 and 1.6). The project's cost was £1,924 2s 9d, this being more than the entire expenditure for draining the rest of the town up to that time. Initially, the prospect of applying sewage from the drain to the land near the outfall was considered to be beneficial.

However, it was not long before the sewage caused an understandable nuisance, which was not satisfactorily overcome until the opening of a municipal sewage works twenty years later.

Details about the drain and tunnel were elaborated upon in typically flowery, melodramatic Victorian style by the *D. N. L. Gaz.* of 29 July 1853:

> If a bountiful supply of pure water is the very fulcrum of all sanitary reform, the most scientific system of drainage and sewerage is of the next importance otherwise there would be such an accumulation of exaggerated cess pools, as would prove detrimental to the public health. The importance of such a system cannot be too highly estimated, as upon it depends, in a great measure, the domestic comfort, cleanliness, and health, and, consequently, the well-being and happiness of the community. The Local Board of Health have not disregarded the value of such a system, in a direction where it was more required than at any former period. A new town has suddenly sprung up in the

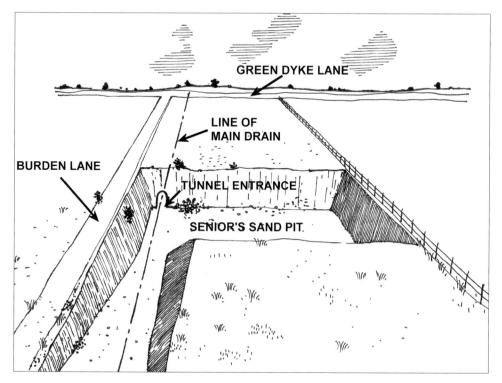

Fig. 1.5 Senior's sand pit with line of main drain.

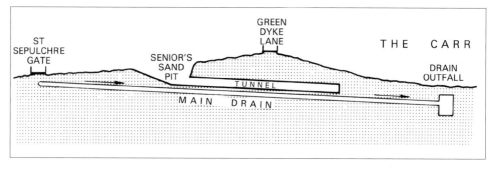

Fig. 1.6 Longitudinal section from St Sepulchre Gate to the Carr.

western portion of the borough. Houses have been multiplied with such marvellous rapidity, the requirements of an increased and increasing population have become daily so pressing, and the demand for further house accommodation has become so much augmented, that an efficient extension of this system is imperatively required. It is, therefore, gratifying to perceive that the necessary steps have been taken to carry it into effect by the formation of a main drain ... Exclusive of the advantages to be derived from this outfall sewer by carrying off the surplus water and contributing to the health and comfort of every dwelling, passage, street, and road in the locality, the capacious tunnel, which will bear the name of "The Rock Sand Tunnel," with its shafts, and wide central excavation, which will be made to resemble a subterranean hall, and fitted up for the reception and accommodation of visitors, will, when completed, be a work of no ordinary character.

The 'sewerage tunnel' aroused much public interest and curiosity, as drainage systems were a novelty at that time. William realised that, when it was completed, he could charge people a small admission fee to inspect it. At the same time he decided to provide an added attraction and tunnelled into the sandstone face on the left of the 'sewerage tunnel' entrance, creating an underground cavern (subsequently named the 'Catacombs') with a vaulted roof, large columns, and numerous intersecting galleries (Fig. 1.7). As William had envisaged, the 'sewerage tunnel' and passages became popular tourist attractions, particularly during the town's annual Race Week. Details of his ideas were documented in the *D. N. L. Gaz.* of 29 July 1853:

Mr Senior, the owner of the [land], will, we understand, spare no expense in [the development of the area]; so that the Rock Sand Tunnel will be fairly deemed one of the "lions of Doncaster," especially when the adjacent "sunken garden," which may be made peculiarly attractive, is laid out in a style somewhat similar to those which adorn the pleasure grounds of the nobility and gentry. When, besides, the crypt, cut also in the rock sand, on the left of the tunnel entrance, with its massive columns and curious passages, receives further extension and adornment, an addition will be made which will much contribute to the peculiar character of the whole extraordinary work; not disregarding, at the same time, the wholesome advantages obtained by carrying out

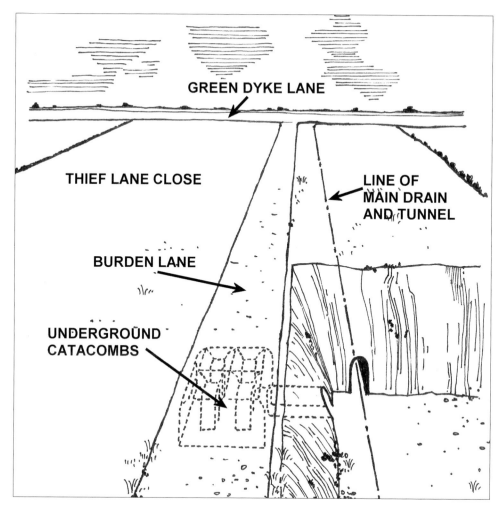

GREEN DYKE LANE

THIEF LANE CLOSE

LINE OF MAIN DRAIN AND TUNNEL

BURDEN LANE

UNDERGROUND CATACOMBS

Fig. 1.7 Artist's impression indicating position of Catacombs.

one of the essential principles intimately connected with the great labours of sanitary improvement, as well as the benefits calculated to be attained in changing the face of old Potteric, and in accelerating its productiveness, by the application of the means placed in the hands of the Local Board of Health.

On 9 September 1853 the *D. N. L. Gaz.* reported on its front page:

Rock Sand Tunnel, Sand Pit House, Sheffield Road, near the Shakespeare's Head. W. Senior announces his intention of throwing open to the Public during the Race Week, the Extraordinary Excavation of the Sand Pit Tunnel, with its Crypt, Grotto &c, and other Works (connected with the Town Drainage), which have excited the wonder of all observers, and will be found interesting to the Race Visitors. Admittance, Sixpence Each.

TO BE SOLD BY PRIVATE TREATY, several
Acres of eligible FREEHOLD BUILDING
GROUND, the most elevated and within the Borough
of Doncaster, in Lots to suit purchasers, considerably
under half price of other vendors.   Apply to Mr
SENIOR, Sheffield Road, Doncaster.
January, 1856.

Fig. 1.8 Advertisement for sale of freehold building ground, January 1856.

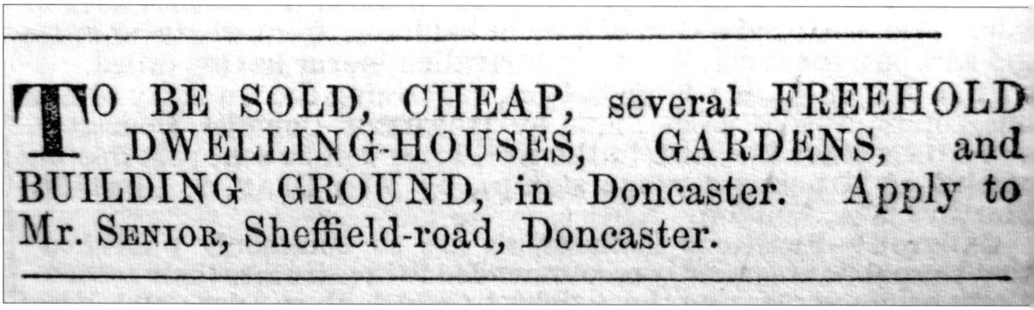

TO BE SOLD, CHEAP, several FREEHOLD
DWELLING-HOUSES, GARDENS, and
BUILDING GROUND, in Doncaster.   Apply to
Mr. SENIOR, Sheffield-road, Doncaster.

Fig. 1.9 Advertisement for sale of houses and building ground, May 1856.

The newspaper also added:

> The Rock Sand Tunnel – We perceive that the Rock Sand Tunnel is announced to be thrown open for inspection of visitors at the races. Amongst the many attractions of the week, this remarkable excavation will not prove the least interesting.

Running concurrently with this drainage development was the establishment of the Great Northern Railway Company's locomotive, carriage and wagon repair works in Doncaster during 1853. Several thousand workers who came to the town from various parts of the country were employed in what became known as the Plant Works. In order to accommodate this influx of people, local landowners sold plots for building purposes. During this period, William Senior acquired substantial areas of land, including over six acres of the district later named Hyde Park, and he began to gain a reputation as a property speculator. On 11 January 1856 and then on 2 May 1856 he placed the above advertisements in the *D. N. L. Gaz.* (Figs 1.8 and 1.9).

We gain an insight into some of William's business methods when C. W. Hatfield, writing a decade later, refers to his development of Hyde Park:

HYDE PARK bears not the slightest resemblance to the fashionable promenade at the west-end of the Metropolis, though the owner of the land, in his arrangement for building sites in 1855 desired to captivate a stray purchaser by its high-sounding appellation. Mr. Senior was, in a local sense, a great speculator; he knew how to chop and exchange, but his bargains were not generally advantageous.

William, as well as selling land for housing, also built houses in various locations. However, in the mid-1850s he embarked upon a project to create a unique house within the sand quarry by a process of excavation and hollowing out of the sandstone. This 'Sand House' evolved in two stages and work on the first part began on the same quarry face that the 'sewerage tunnel' entrance was situated. As the land was excavated in the direction of Green Dyke Lane, a massive sandstone block was left in situ adjacent to Burden Lane. From this block the first section of the house was carved, with part of the 'sewerage tunnel' forming an arched passageway alongside it. The first part of the house was completed *c.* 1857, was spread over two storeys and had four rooms (Fig. 1.10).

On 15 May 1858 the *Illustrated London News* drew the public's attention to a large and magnificent fungus growing in the 'sewerage tunnel's' remaining section. Local artist Henry Tilbury made a drawing of the specimen (*Hydnum barba-Jovis,* or Jove's Beard), which was depicted in the magazine (Fig. 1.11).

Although the fungus' proportions are somewhat exaggerated in the drawing, an impression of the tunnel at this time can nevertheless be gained. Tilbury also provided the following description:

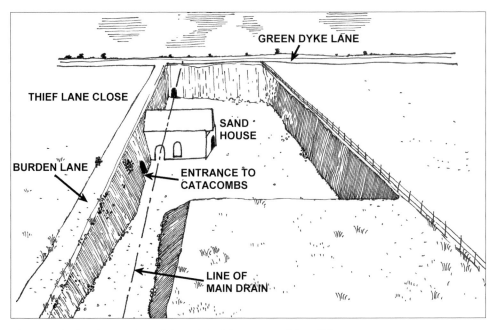

Fig. 1.10 Artist's impression of the original four-roomed Sand House.

GREAT FUNGUS IN A TUNNEL NEAR DONCASTER.

Fig. 1.11 The Great Fungus in the 'sewerage tunnel.'

The fungus has been growing for twelve months, and is still growing. It now measures fifteen feet [4.6 m] in diameter. It is of the most beautiful lacework description. It grows from a piece of timber in the roof of a tunnel, and branches off in every direction till it forms an elegant border of rich white fringe, spangled all over in a most beautiful manner with water drops.

Local botanist and Linnean Society member Samuel Appleby published a similar description of the fungus in the *D. N. L. Gaz.* of 16 April 1858:

It is growing in a cave or tunnel, probably a hundred yards from the entrance, and the atmosphere in the part where it grows differing little in winter from summer; always dark, invariably damp, and constantly temperate; that the plant can increase in size until the source from whence its nourishment was first obtained becomes exhausted, and that does not seem to be the case until it reaches an enormous size, far beyond any former prescribed limits; increasing progressively and regularly; and besides the original roof, sandstone surface may also afford nutriment to perpetuate its health, so that a continued growth is the consequence ... Mr Henry Senior, who lives in the Castellated Rock House, will gladly facilitate the curious visitor. And, by the by, the Rock House is worth seeing – a house cut purely out of the solid sandstone rock. Such a dwelling might have been expected by a visitor to Petrea, but in this place is quite a novelty, and no description will be equal to that of beholding the place itself.

Within only twenty-five years of William Senior acquiring Balby Lane Close, his business activities had developed from market gardening into commercial sand supply and property speculation, taking full advantage of Doncaster's expansion and development. The arrival of major industry thus occurred at the same time as the inception of the Sand House, and may indeed have acted as a catalyst in its creation.

In the last two years of his life William displayed elements of unusual behaviour which bordered on the eccentric. The *D. N. L. Gaz.* of 1 May 1857 reported that William was charged with assault:

ASSAULT. – Mr. William Senior, of the Sand-pits, Balby-road, was summoned by Mrs. Harriet Mountain, wife of Mr. Joseph Mountain, grocer, for an assault on Monday last. Mr C. E. Palmer supported the complaint, and Mr Marratt appeared for Mr. Senior. – Mrs. Mountain said that she had occasion to go towards a field belonging to the defendant to fetch an Australian magpie which had strayed from her house. Whilst going on the occupation road the defendant approached and asked her where she was going. She said that she wanted her bird, as last Saturday Mr. Henry Senior had been complaining of it. Defendant told her he could not allow her to go for it that way – she must take another road; and she turned back. He said he could not allow her after what had previously occurred. She supposed this to refer to a quarrel which defendant had had last summer with her husband. The defendant used very abusive language to her, and raised a shovel to strike her. He then threw two shovelfuls of sand at her. – Cross-examined by Mr MARRATT: The magpie was of the Australian breed, and was very fierce. She had two of them, and they had got into the habit of trespassing upon Mr. Senior's land. She had made use of a very vulgar expression to the defendant at the time he was raising the shovel to strike her. – Mr PALMER called one of Mr. Senior's workmen to support the complaint. He, however, denied that the shovel was raised to strike her. – Mr MARRATT, in reply, said the assault was not proved, and that Mrs. Mountain's tongue and magpies were a nuisance to her neighbours, and if any one was bound to keep the peace it ought to be the magpies. Mrs. Mountain's magpies were continually trespassing, and she was about to do the same herself when the defendant would not allow her, whereupon she became very

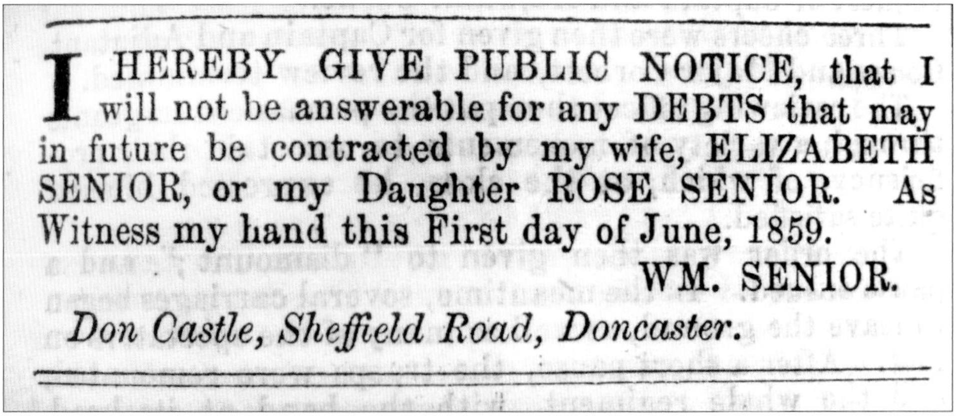

I HEREBY GIVE PUBLIC NOTICE, that I will not be answerable for any DEBTS that may in future be contracted by my wife, ELIZABETH SENIOR, or my Daughter ROSE SENIOR. As Witness my hand this First day of June, 1859.

WM. SENIOR.

Don Castle, Sheffield Road, Doncaster.

Fig. 1.12 Public Notice from William Senior.

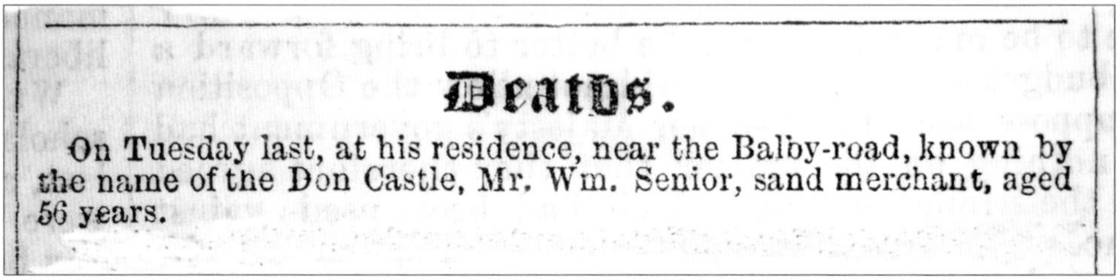

Deaths.

On Tuesday last, at his residence, near the Balby-road, known by the name of the Don Castle, Mr. Wm. Senior, sand merchant, aged 56 years.

Fig. 1.13 Notice of William Senior's death.

abusive, and the defendant might or might not throw a shovelful of sand upon her. She had brought the whole upon herself, and was solely to blame. He therefore asked for the summons to be dismissed. – The bench having heard witnesses who spoke to the language used by the complainant, the MAYOR said the summons would be dismissed, as they were of opinion that no assault would have been made had not provocation been first given. – Case dismissed.

On 3 June 1859 the same newspaper carried a notice from William (Fig. 1.12).

William Senior died on the 5 July 1859 and, frustratingly, no obituary appeared for him in the local newspaper, only a mention in the list of deaths in the *D. N. L. Gaz.* of 8 July 1859 (Fig. 1.13).

Chapter Two

Henry Senior
and the Sand House

Fig. 2.1 Statue of 'Summer.'

HENRY SENIOR AND THE SAND HOUSE

Henry Senior returned to Doncaster *c.* 1853. Various deeds relating to that year and the following one record that he was a coal dealer. However, on the birth certificate of his second daughter, Emma, who was born on 6 December 1856, he is recorded as being a gardener and living in Alma Terrace. The reasons for Henry's removal from Barnsley and, indeed, why he had actually ventured there in the first instance, are unknown, although it should be noted that his wife Mary originated from the Barnsley area. It is, however, tempting to suggest that, as he was the eldest son, he had returned to help run his ageing father's various expanding business ventures.

In the 1858 *I. L. N.* article about the 'sewerage tunnel' fungus, Henry is mentioned as living in the 'castellated Rock House' (see Fig. 2.2, which illustrates the castellated effect on the balcony of the house's west gable). The fact that Henry was living in the Sand House at this time not only reveals that he had moved from Alma Terrace, but also raises the question, was it William or Henry who was responsible for the house's conception? Although it can be argued that William, in his role as head of the family business, ought to have taken any major decisions regarding the house's evolution, he is only noted as living there during the last year of his life. In contrast, Henry appears to have moved into the house as soon as the first portion was completed. In fact, the part of the sand pit containing the Sand House was bought by Henry from William in April 1857 and a conveyance for the property refers to the 'tenement ... cut out of rock sand, lately converted by Henry Senior into a dwelling house'. Whether it was William or Henry who actually originated the idea for the Sand House will probably never be known, and it is perhaps diplomatic to suggest that it was the brainchild of both father and son.

The *Doncaster Review* of August 1894 also avoids the question of the original creator of the Sand House – if indeed it was one person – by not stating which Mr Senior (William or Henry) they are referring to in the article: 'The Sand Rock House at Doncaster':

> While excavating the sand, Mr Senior – who, if he had not been in business, would have
> made his mark either as an architect or an artist – conceived the idea of making himself

Fig. 2.2 Sand House gable.

a house out of the rock sand. After drawing his plans and making his calculations, he and his sons set to work, and gradually the house began to assume shape. The work took time, the sand had to be carefully removed, and the craftsmen engaged must have been endowed with rare patience and must have exercised considerable skill...

Evidence of Henry's increasing involvement with his father's business affairs can be found in 1859, when both men are mentioned in a draft conveyance relating to the purchase of a parcel of land known as Thief Lane Close. They acquired this property for the sum of £1,705 at an auction held only days before William's death.

The high price paid was regarded by the *D. N. L. Gaz.* as 'extraordinary' since the reserve price on the land was only £900. Thief Lane Close, part of which had belonged to the Trustees of St Thomas's Hospital, was situated to the east of the Seniors' property; the two areas of land were separated by Burden Lane. As Thief Lane Close could have been used for building purposes or excavated for moulding sand, acquiring this conveniently situated area was crucial to the growth of the Senior family's business interests and, ultimately, the expansion of the Sand House. Furthermore, this perhaps explains why an unexpectedly large sum of money was paid for the land by the Seniors.

Speculation that Henry's reason for returning from Barnsley in the 1850s was to help his father run his businesses is further consolidated when it is learned that, upon William's death in 1859, he left everything to Henry, who by this time was his only surviving child. Indeed, Henry was the first born of William's nine children and he out-lived all his brothers and sisters. He was also William's only child to survive beyond the age of thirty. The 1861 Census, and Kelly's *Post Office Directory* for the same year, note that Henry was a sand merchant living at Rock House on the Sheffield Road. A year earlier, a local newspaper had noted him as the Alma Inn's owner. This property was situated a short distance away from the Sand House, at the junction of Burden Lane and St Sepulchre Gate. The inn's exact opening date is unknown but it is likely to have been between 1854, when the Battle of the Alma took place in the Crimea (after which the inn was probably named) and 1860, which is the earliest located reference.

In 1863 Henry obtained permission from the Local Board of Health (1 January 1863), to carry out several schemes in Thief Lane Close. One of these involved the building of a row of houses at the Close's south end, facing Green Dyke Lane. Another was centred on the formation of two new roads across the land. Throughout the previous decade a short cul-de-sac had existed, known as Victoria Street, which ran southwards from St James' Street and terminated at the northern boundary of Thief Lane Close. One of Henry's new roads formed an extension to Victoria Street, continuing southwards through the Close to Green Dyke Lane. The second new road lay at right angles to the first one, in the north-west corner of the Close. The formation of a new thoroughfare between St James' Street/St Sepulchre Gate and Green Dyke Lane (i.e. Victoria Street and its extension) effectively made Burden Lane redundant and, therefore, Henry was granted permission to close it. Thus the original and the newly-acquired areas of Senior land were united. Housing developments that Henry

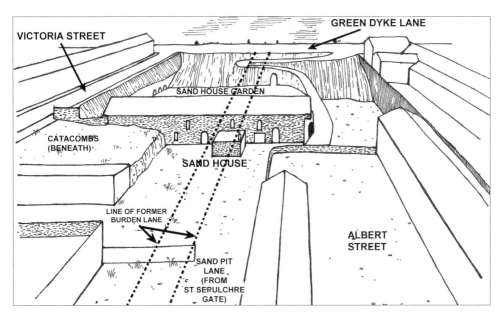

Fig. 2.3 Artist's impression of the completed Sand House *c.* 1880.

subsequently carried out along the Victoria Street extension were initially called Senior Terrace, New Senior Terrace and Senior Street, but ultimately the entire road took the name Victoria Street.

One of the conditions stipulated by the Local Board of Health before granting permission for these developments was that Henry must not excavate within five yards of the new roads. However, this still allowed Burden Lane to be excavated and the sand quarry to be extended eastwards. Henry also planned to extend the Catacombs and link them to a tunnel to be excavated beneath Victoria Street. The Local Board of Health approved the proposal for the tunnel, which would be 2.4 m (8 feet) wide and 9 m (30 feet) below street level.

All the 1863 Board-approved schemes are thought to have been completed by the early 1870s. Details of the development of the Catacombs and the new tunnel beneath Victoria Street are included in the next chapter. Disappointingly, no references have been located concerning permission to extend the Sand House, or details about its eventual completion. Clearly the house must have undergone major development around the same time as the other schemes mentioned. The house's first section originally abutted Burden Lane, but when the quarry's eastern face progressed through and beyond the lane, a new addition to the premises was created. This extension was carried out by excavating the sandstone from in and around it, the same process having earlier been used to form the house's original part. The fact that no references to the house's development have been found in the Board of Health minutes or local newspapers is somewhat puzzling and frustrating. Information in local newspapers, however, was rather limited at this time, and reports concerning private individuals, other than if they were involved with criminal activities, were rare. A possible though

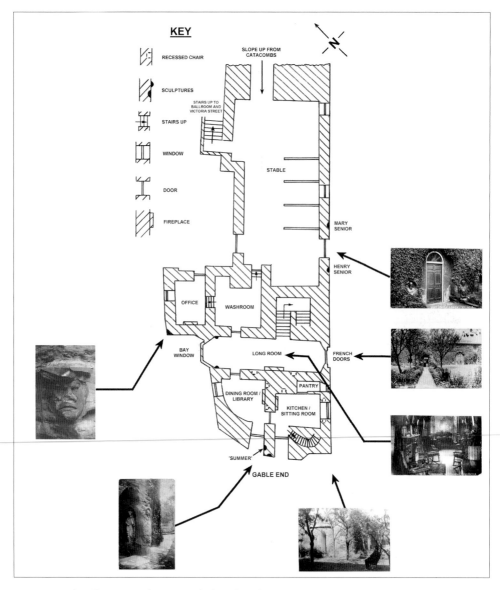

Fig. 2.4 Lower floor room layout with thumbnails.

tenuous explanation for the lack of details might be that, apart from the roof, the Sand House was not actually built, but hewn out of solid rock. It may not, therefore, have been subject to the planning regulations of the day. An impression of how the area appeared by 1880 is given by Fig. 2.3, and this should be compared with Fig. 1.10.

Before giving details about the completed Sand House it is worthwhile noting several incidental events which occurred while the main developments were taking place. In 1869 the Local Board of Health resolved that the town's sewage should no longer be deposited on the Carr, as it had been causing a nuisance for some years. Consequently,

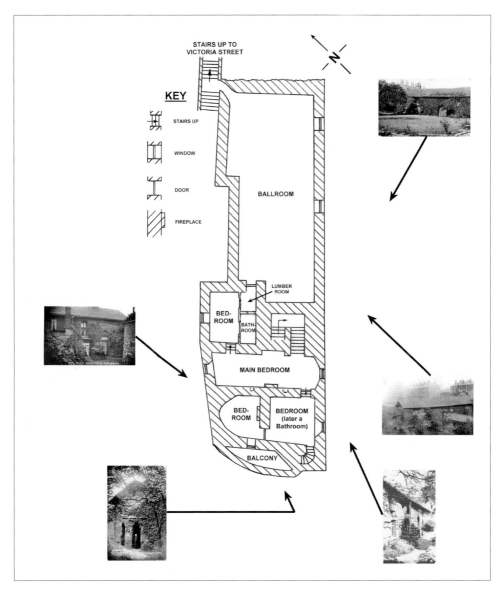

Fig. 2.5 Upper floor room layout with thumbnails.

from April 1873, sewage was pumped to a new sewage works at Sandall, north-east of Doncaster. The original drain, which ran beneath the Sand House, was then utilised to carry only surface water, a function it still performs at the time of writing.

As well as owning the Alma Inn, Henry is also noted in 1870 as possessing a Marsh Gate beer house, the Labour in Vain, which he subsequently rebuilt. The 1871 Census shows Henry and his family living at the Alma Inn, with the Sand House being unoccupied, possibly as a result of extensive alterations taking place.

Fig. 2.6 The Long Room, pre-1900.

By this time Arthur, the eldest of Henry and Mary's five children (a sixth had died in infancy) was twenty years old. He was already a foreman in the sand business, thus allowing his father to devote more time to his various property interests.

Although Henry was involved in many projects in the 1860s and 1870s, completing the Sand House must surely have been the one he most enjoyed. By then the house's length was 37 m (120 feet) and its width 13 m (42 feet). Some of the outer walls were 2.7 m (9 feet) thick and the inner walls 0.9 m (3 feet). No original internal layout

Fig. 2.7 Recessed chair to the left of the Long Room fireplace.

SAND CHAIR,

SAND HOUSE, DONCASTER. No 1.

plans have been discovered, but Figs 2.4 and 2.5 show each floor's arrangement, based on information compiled from Ordnance Survey plans, newspaper descriptions and various individuals' personal recollections. There were ten habitable rooms, the largest being the ballroom, which could reputedly accommodate 300 people. Below the ballroom was a stable block. The four rooms (two on each floor) and winding staircase at the west end comprised the original house. An earth closet was located in the garden. The arched passageway, which was formerly part of the 'sewerage tunnel' and which separated the original Sand House from Burden Lane, was converted into the Long Room. It was formed by fixing a bay window at one end and French doors at the other. Fig. 2.6 shows three unidentified people seated in the Long Room and it is just possible to distinguish figures carved at either side of the window.

The room's walls were partially panelled; other walls and the ceilings in the house were plastered. Recessed chairs and the Long Room's fireplace are pictured in Figs 2.7 and 2.8. The house's outer walls were 'topped off' by a few courses of brickwork surmounted by a pantile roof.

The main entrance in the west gable was 'guarded' by a figure named 'Summer' (Fig. 2.9). Conventional window casements and doors were fixed, while inside the house cupboards were cut out of the sand, as were the recessed seats incorporating Gothic arches. The staircase was hewn out of rock, while smoke from the fires rose through sandstone chimneys. Figs 2.10, 2.11 and 2.12 show general views of the house's exterior and Fig. 2.13 details of the front stable door, with busts reputedly of Henry and Mary at either side.

Tomlinson in *From Doncaster into Hallamshire c.* 1870 gives information about the house:

> The sand for about three acres, to the depth of nearly forty feet [12m] (the bed goes much lower, but could not be profitably worked on account of the water), has been excavated and carted away, leaving a perpendicular mound. This, from a quaint idea, and with immense labour, has been hewn and cut into a dwelling, containing ten rooms.

Fig. 2.8 Fireplace and recessed chairs in Long Room.

Right: Fig. 2.9 Statue of 'Summer.'

Below: Fig. 2.10 Carving on office corner.

Fig. 2.11 Back of Sand House.

Fig. 2.12 Panoramic view of Sand House area from Green Dyke Lane, *c.* 1900.

Fig. 2.13 Stable door and carvings of Henry and Mary Senior.

The *Don. Gaz.* of 2 August 1912 added further details:

> Remembering always that we were standing in rooms every cubic inch of which was
> hewn out of the solid sandstone, the interior of the house seemed almost worthy to
> be ranked as the eighth wonder of the world. There was nothing primitive about
> it, nothing suggesting a return to the habits of life of the troglodytes. Everything
> had been planned according to the ideas of a man who believed in comfort and had
> definite ideas of taste in ornament...

In looking for a motive behind the Sand House's creation J. F. W. Lyons, in his article
'Castle of Sand was in Quarry', published in the *Don. Gaz.* 29 June 1961, offers the
following:

> Now Sandy [presumably he meant Henry] was an 'off beat' individual ... It is said
> that he was a victim of chronic toothache and insomnia, and either affliction in ample
> doses is enough to send anybody "up the wall." But in Sandy's case, the reaction
> seemed to have an opposite effect. As a believer in the dictum that hard work will
> cure all ails, it caused him to seek relief in burrowing underground. In consequence
> of this nocturnal activity, when he died he left behind a remarkable memorial – an
> architectural oddity known as 'Sand Rock Castle ...'

Fig. 2.14 Front garden looking north towards Long Room.

Lyons also pondered on the sheer logistics of creating the Sand House:

> Just what a colossal task it must have been for a man to excavate such a place can be better appreciated in remembering that a hundred years ago, there were no such things as mechanical diggers and bulldozers, and the task must have involved considerable pick and shovel work.

The *Doncaster Review* article of August 1894 also stated:

> Numbers of people living in Doncaster travel miles to see "the sights" of other towns and places, and yet never make an effort to become acquainted with their own town and neighbourhood ... we do not think there is anything to equal [the Sand House] in the whole of England.

Once the sand quarry had been extended as far as Victoria Street and Green Dyke Lane, it was effectively exhausted, allowing it to be converted into a 'sunken' garden. The area was arranged with paths and lawns, and was extensively planted, as illustrated by Fig. 2.14. An abundance of ivy covered the house's front, fruit trees flourished and even a vine was grown against the quarry face beneath Victoria Street. Indeed, the house and its environs were exceedingly well-appointed, and any image of a primitive, cave-like dwelling conjured up by the name Sand House cannot be further from the truth. A view looking north-east, with the figure on the right allegedly being Henry Senior, supports this opinion (Fig. 2.15).

Fig. 2.15 Figure, allegedly Henry Senior, seated in garden; gable to the left.

In 1875 the marriage took place between Henry's daughter, Emma and a miner's son, William Hemingway, who was from Clay Cross, in Derbyshire. William played an important part in the Sand House story over the following four decades, as noted in Chapter 5.

Five years after his daughter's marriage, Henry was elected as a councillor to represent Doncaster's West Ward, the votes being: Senior 610; Elwiss 551; Durrans 467; Benton 414; Pevey 75; Smith 35. This was his own locality, being bounded by Green Dyke Lane, St Sepulchre Gate, High Street, Hall Gate, South Parade, Bennetthorpe and Hyde Park. During the following three years he sat on the Bye-Law, Finance, Market, Sanitary and School Attendance Committees. Although he was a regular attendee at council meetings, the minute books do not reveal that he made any major contribution to local politics. At the expiry of his three year term of office he failed to be re-elected, the figures being: Bentley 1148; Robinson 775; Milnthorp 487; Senior 375.

The 1881 Census notes that all except one of Henry and Mary's children had left the Sand House, although they continued to live locally. In September 1882, at the age of sixty-two, Mary Senior (Fig. 2.16) died. Subsequently, Emily Clara Whitehead, a former servant girl in the Sand House, became Henry's second wife.

A strange report in the *Don. Gaz.* of 22 June 1883 detailed alleged sightings of an apparition at the Sand House:

AN ALLEGED GHOST AT DONCASTER. – If all be true that has lately been said, Doncaster is now the habitation of a ghost, and the Sand-house and its vicinity is

Fig. 2.16 Mary Senior *c*. 1880.

its chosen locality. Hundreds and hundreds at night time during the last week have assembled to get a glimpse of the supernatural visitor, and although some have alleged to have seen the intruder, none have so far brought it to bay. The origin of this ghost is singular indeed. According to rumour, on Thursday or Friday night last, the occupant of the Sand-house fancied he heard someone walking on the outside. He let the dog loose, and then, feeling secure, he looked out in the dark only to see the form of a woman all clothed in white. Knowing that the dog must be somewhere about, he put out his hand to push the figure away, when, lo and behold, it vanished into the earth, and the person who had seen it as quickly vanished into his house. The next day others were informed of the visit, and for nights afterwards crowds assembled in the locality to see the ghost return. Some of these have professed to have seen what they went to witness, but the majority believe it is only a creation of the man's imagination.

A week later, the same newspaper carried a story headed 'The Rumour of a Ghost at the Sand House' (Fig. 2.17).

THE RUMOUR OF A GHOST AT THE SAND HOUSE.—
Mr. Hy. Senior desires us to say that the rumour
mentioned in our paragraph of Friday last, has no
foundation whatever. We are glad to give Mr.
Senior's denial, as such will tend more than anything
to prevent the circulation of the story in future.

Fig. 2.17 'Rumour of ghost' newspaper article, 29 June 1883.

On 22 March 1887, Henry's new wife Emily bore him a son, and in celebration of
Queen Victoria's Golden Jubilee, the baby was given the grand name of Henry Jubilee
Whitehead Senior. Sadly he survived for only a few months.

Throughout the 1880s and into the 1890s Henry's interest in the licensed trade
continued with his ownership of the 'Don Castle Brewery'. This was initially housed
in a building in The Backway (now Market Road), but it was later transferred a few
yards to a more prominent position in the Market Place. Although Henry was the
Brewery's owner, it was managed by his son Arthur, who had reputedly been forced to
leave the sand business after suffering a serious injury when working.

As previously mentioned, we are not certain that we possess any images of either
William or Henry Senior. However, it has been stated by various family members that
the younger man in both Figs 2.18 and 2.19 is Henry. No clear indication has been
given as to the identity of the other gentleman.

Henry's property dealings were virtually over by 1891, when, at the age of sixty-six,
he seems to have retired from business. This is illustrated by only two land transactions
being registered in his name after this date, compared with eighty in the previous four
decades.

The first detailed article describing the Sand House appeared in the *Doncaster
Review* of 1894. It revealed that the house and tunnels had been open for inspection
for years, but lamented:

> The great drawback hitherto has been that the approach to the place was a very bad
> one, but that reproach will shortly be removed. The Corporation and the Rural Sanitary
> Authority have lately made Green Dyke Lane into quite a respectable thoroughfare,
> and there will be no more "fishing" there in pools that stood in the roadway for almost
> as long as the "oldest inhabitant" could remember. We understand that Mr. Senior
> intends to make the principal entrance to his grounds from this new road, and the
> visitor will gradually descend an incline until he is on the level of the house…

The article states that in Henry's younger days he spent much time painting in oils.
Examples of his work, as well as pictures by old masters, adorned the house. The piece
concluded by stating:

Above left: Fig. 2.18 Figures seated outside the Long Room.

Above right: Fig. 2.19 Figures seated in the front garden.

[Henry] and his son, George Senior, and his son-in-law, Mr. Hemingway, are constantly making improvements and additions to what is really the wonder of the neighbourhood.

This period was undoubtedly the Sand House's heyday. Dances were held regularly, in the ballroom during the winter and in the sunken garden in the summer. Guests could alight from their carriages and enter the ballroom via a flight of stairs leading directly from Victoria Street. The well-known Doncaster tradesman and musician A. B. Dodds, reminiscing about his past life, stated that back in the 1890s he used to run the weekly dances that were held at the Sand House when 'the curious dwelling was a place of resort'. During the winter months the dances took place in a large room under the roof of the Sand House itself, but on the summer evenings dancing was upon the 'greensward in the sunk garden adjoining, which was bedecked with fairy lights quite in carnival style'. An undated handbill, arguably from this period, is seen in Fig. 2.20.

In the corner of the lawn a platform was erected, and on this Mr Dodds had his band – a harp, violin, clarinet and cornet. During an interval in the programme the company had the opportunity of going through the tunnel and inspecting its curious carvings,

OPEN DAILY,

From 6 p.m. to 9 p.m., 6d. each. Thursdays from 2 p.m to 9 p.m., 1/- each, also all Holidays, 6d, each.

TO BE SEEN

AT

MR. H. SENIOR'S,

Near the Shakesphere's Head; on the Sheffield Road, the

DON CASTLE

CAVERN,

GROTTO TUNNEL,

(1000 yards, lighted with gas), cut out of the solid Rock ; also the extraordinary

FUNGUSES,

Now growing in the Tunnel, as well as several others in the different stages of developement.

Visitors are requested not to Touch the Models.

Thwaites & Co., Printers, Doncaster.

Fig. 2.20 Handbill advertising Don Castle.

and Mr Dodds assured everyone that these al fresco dances of the late Victorian period 'often attracted very goodly gatherings'.

Worthy of note is the following advertisement which appeared in the *Don. Gaz.* of 23 April 1897:

> Sand House, Don Castle Pleasure Ground. Open Good Friday, Easter Monday and every Thursday during Summer. Band and large platform for dancing. Also on view Grotto Tunnel 6000 yds – lighted with gas – cut out of solid rock – extraordinary Fungi in the different stages of development, open from 2 until dusk, 6d each. Refreshments at popular prices.

In August of the same year 250 residents of Victoria and Cambridge Streets celebrated Queen Victoria's Diamond Jubilee at a gathering held in the Sand House grounds as recorded in the *Don. Gaz.* 13 August 1897:

> Jubilee Celebrations. Victoria and Cambridge Streets. The dwellers in the above-named streets held their joint jubilee celebrations on Thursday evening last week, the site of the festivities being the Don Castle pleasure grounds, kindly lent for the occasion by Mr Senior. These two streets which are in the neighbourhood of the above place of recreation, were decorated in a manner worthy of such an event. Tea was provided for both children and adults, the Co-operative Stores having the honour of catering ... The children were slightly in the majority ... At 7.30 the fete was enlivened by selections of music ably rendered by the Borough Band, which kept up its performance till midnight. During the evening, in addition to the Band, those present were entertained by the sight of the grotto and fungi, for which the Don Castle is so famous. In addition to these sights, so pleasing to the eye, refreshments were served out during the evening through the kindness of Mrs Senior. All thoroughly enjoyed themselves both at tea and during the evening, those who went into the grounds after tea being delighted with the music and sights of the grounds especially the tunnel

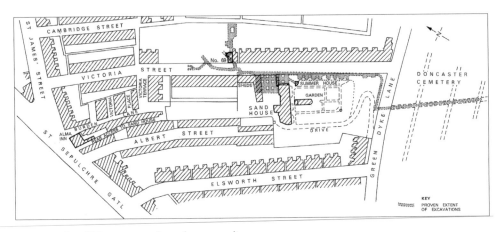

Fig. 2.21 Sand House, tunnels and surrounding area *c.* 1900.

Public Notices.

MR. SENIOR, Sand House, returns thanks to the kind friends who assisted him into Mr. Haresign's Garden after his misfortune; especially Mr. Wood and Mrs. Haresign, who were so kind in bathing his contusions.

Above: Fig. 2.22 Public notice from Henry Senior, 23 July 1897.

Right: Fig. 2.23 Henry Senior's funeral card.

In Loving Memory

In Loving Memory of

HENRY,

The dearly beloved Husband of Clara Emma Senior,

Who fell asleep in Jesus April 1st, 1900,

AGED 74 YEARS.

Interred at Doncaster Cemetery, April 4th.

Sudden was the death of me,
And great surprise to all;
When God did say I must away
Could I refuse the call.

" Behold He taketh away, who can hinder Him? Who will say unto Him what doest Thou?"—Job, chap. ix, v. 12.

which was lighted up during the evening. Mr Senior, on his appearance at half past ten was greeted with a loud burst of cheering...

By the end of the nineteenth century the area around the Sand House had become completely built up and was largely populated by railway workers. Fig. 2.21 clearly positions the house and tunnels in relation to the surrounding streets.

Evidence that Henry's health was beginning to fail is given in a notice which he placed in the *Don. Gaz.* 23 July 1897 (Fig. 2.22).

Henry had led a full and active life for seventy-four years when, on 1 April 1900, he passed away. His funeral card is shown in Fig. 2.23. Details surrounding his death are recorded in his obituary published in the *Doncaster Chronicle* of 6 April 1900:

Mr. Henry Senior, sand merchant, of Sand House, Balby Road, died on Sunday last, at the ripe old age of 74. He was out on the Thursday, but was taken ill on the same day with a very bad attack of bronchitis, to which he was somewhat predisposed and pneumonia supervened.

Henry was buried in the family's plain, uninscribed vault (Fig. 2.24) adjacent to Doncaster (later known as Hyde Park) Cemetery chapel. The vault was only a short distance from the unique dwelling which he had occupied for over forty years.

Henry devised his will in 1895, five years prior to his death. He instructed his executors, Thomas Henry Berry, a rent collector, and William Hemingway, his son-in-law, to sell all his belongings upon his decease. The *Don. Chron.* of 15 June 1900 gave details of the sale of the estate:

Sand House, Doncaster.
Mr Henry Senior, Deceased.
Household Furniture, Building Material, and Effects.

Messrs J. Dawson & Sons have received instructions from the Trustees of Mr Henry Senior, deceased, to Sell By Auction, on the premises, Sand House, Doncaster, on Wednesday, 27th June, 1900, the valuable Household Furniture, Building Material, Horse, Cart, Phaeton, Harness, Trade Implements, and Effects, viz.,

Building Materials, &c at 12 o'clock prompt.

100 bundles of laths, 80 doors, 100 various sanitary pipes, ridge tiles, plinth bricks, a quantity of new and second-hand bricks and fire bricks, navvy barrows, planks and scaffold poles, 6 iron-barred window frames, and a quantity of frames and sashes, a number of ranges, range fronts and hobs, 3½ gross of sash weights, a quantity of new rails and styles for doors, 10 flights of old stairs, a quantity of stone and marble, including sills, jambs, sinks and slabs, old wood and firewood. About 100 yards of Tramway Rails with 4 Corves on wheels.

Outside Effects.

3-horse power Engine and horizontal boiler, 2 chaff cutters, potato steamer and boiler complete, weighing machine and weights, 2 wringing machines, wood poultry houses and runs, corn bins, dog kennel, Phaeton with cushions, Cart with shelvings,

Fig. 2.24 The Senior family vault in Hyde Park Cemetery, Doncaster.

set of light Harness, set of Cart Harness, brown Horse Tommy, 7 years old, 6 couples of Fowls, 9 Pigeons.

Furniture, &c at 2 o'clock.

Mahogany hair seated suite, comprising couch, arm chair, lady's chair, rocking chair and 6 small chairs; inlaid walnut cabinet, walnut overmantel, 2 oval walnut tables, inlaid draft table, 4 fold screen, Axminster carpet and hearthrug, 2 large vases, 2 Etruscan vases, cornice poles, rings and curtains, mahogany secretaire, mahogany dining table with 2 extra leaves, pier glass, mahogany arm chair, 2 small chairs, brass ashes pan, fenders and fireirons, black plaster figure, oak chest of drawers, mahogany round table, sewing machine, Windsor chair, couch, barometer, office desks and drawers, 2 kitchen tables, wood chairs, loose bath, gas stove, invalid's folding chair, a quantity of **Oil Paintings**, including landscape by Tilbury; Pictures and Ornamental Books, &c.

Handsome brass half-tester bedstead with wings, with plush and chintz curtains, and furniture and spring mattress, chest of drawers, with painted figures, night commode, mahogany wardrobe with plate glass front, marble top wash stand, dressing table with fixed toilet glass and jewel drawers, papier maché table, toilet ware, square mantel glass, 4 post bedstead with furniture, dressing tables, wash stands, mahogany cane seated chairs, 6 chairs in American leather, wood bedstead, feather beds, bolsters and pillows, carpets and hearthrugs, blankets, sheets, counter-panes, and linen, kitchen utensils, Crockery, Glass, &c.

A quantity of **Plants** in pots.

Sale to commence with the Building Material and Outside Effects at 12 o'clock prompt; Furniture at 2 o'clock.

Auctioneer's Offices – St George Gate, Doncaster.

The proceeds of the sale were then divided according to Henry's precise instructions amongst his wife and three surviving children. Henry's wishes also included the sale of the Sand House. Consequently, on 20 August 1900, four months after his death, the Sand House and its grounds were conveyed to Doncaster Corporation for the sum of £1,000.

Chapter Three

The Tunnels
and Carvings

Fig. 3.1 'Pat' the Irishman.

THE TUNNELS AND CARVINGS

At this point a departure will be made from the Sand House's chronological story to take a more detailed look at the tunnels which emanated from the house and the carvings that adorned them. Initially, it is necessary to reiterate where the various underground excavations were located. Once Burden Lane had been removed and the sand quarry had reached its full extent, little remained of the original 'sewerage tunnel'. Only the short section through the house (i.e. the Long Room) and a 90 m (300 foot) length from Green Dyke Lane southwards, still existed. The Catacombs, which William Senior had excavated in the early 1850s to attract the public, had been somewhat altered by this stage. It should be noted that a certain amount of doubt exists regarding the precise size and position of William's Catacombs. Entry to the Catacombs from the original sand pit was described by the *D. N. L. Gaz.* of 29 July 1853 as being to the left of the 'sewerage tunnel'. This placed them either directly below Burden Lane or slightly further east, beneath Thief Lane Close. As the close was not in Senior ownership at the time, it is assumed that William's Catacombs were actually beneath Burden Lane (Fig. 1.7). However, the removal of Burden Lane must have resulted in the disappearance of the original Catacombs. This is quite feasible, but it means that the later Catacombs, which existed during the latter part of the nineteenth century, had completely replaced William's original excavations, they being further to the east and partially beneath Victoria Street (Fig. 2.21).

Reference has already been made to the tunnel situated below the west side of Victoria Street, for which Henry Senior obtained authorisation in 1863. This tunnel ran from the Catacombs parallel to, and about 5 m (16 feet) behind, the rock face at the sand quarry's east side. Eight short cross-tunnels, or adits, extended from the main tunnel, terminating with windows where the adits met the rock face (Fig. 3.2). The windows illuminated the tunnel and gave it a monastic appearance, hence the name 'Cloisters' being adopted for this section. Furthermore, when the quarry was landscaped, glimpses of it could be seen from the Cloisters. At the Cloisters' southern end, the tunnel turned in a westerly direction to follow the line of Green Dyke Lane, until it met what remained of the 'sewerage tunnel,' heading towards the cemetery.

Fig. 3.2 Cross section through the Cloisters, looking south.

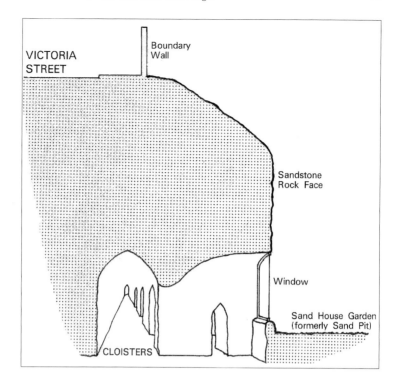

While the Cloisters led southwards from the Catacombs, another tunnel left this area and extended north, then divided into several branches. It is known that one of these gave access to a large cavern beneath the rear yard of No. 69 Victoria Street, the home of Henry's son-in-law William Hemingway. This cavern will be described in a later chapter. The extent of the other branches is unknown, but it is possible that at least one of them led to another sand quarry, which the 25-inch scale Ordnance Survey map of 1892 shows as lying to the east of Victoria Street, north of No. 69.

The overall proven length of the tunnel from north to south was 280 m (920 feet). However, many myths have developed over the years concerning the extent of the workings. These include references to one tunnel entering the Senior burial vault and the cemetery chapel crypt, while another is claimed to have run to the Shakespeare Dock (a nearby railway goods depot); overall lengths of up to 6000 yards have been quoted, but no evidence has been found to substantiate these claims.

After detailing where the Catacombs and Cloisters were situated, the authors will now take the reader on an imaginary exploration of the tunnels as they were in the late nineteenth century. The journey will commence at the Sand House itself, and proceed via the Catacombs to the Cloisters before returning to the summer house in the garden.

We enter the Sand House through the stable's front door and turn to the right where a ramp slopes down into the Catacombs. This section is approximately 28 m (90 feet) long by 17 m (55 feet) wide and a high vaulted roof is supported by massive, rectangular sandstone columns. The lack of natural light gives the place a ghostly character and it

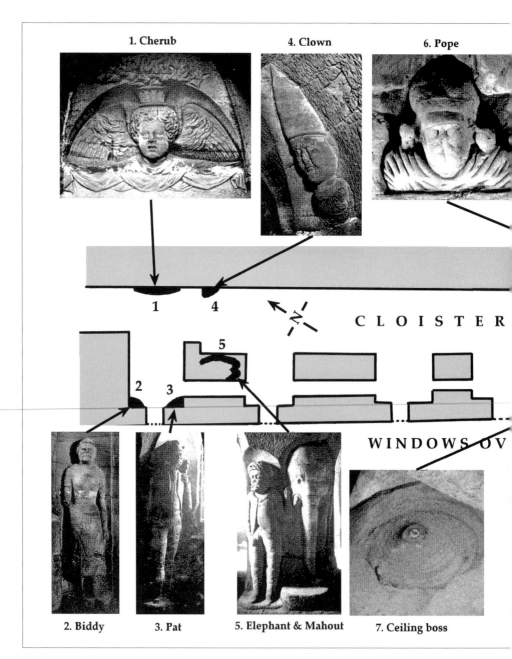

Fig. 3.3 Plan of Cloisters, illustrating major carvings with thumbnails.

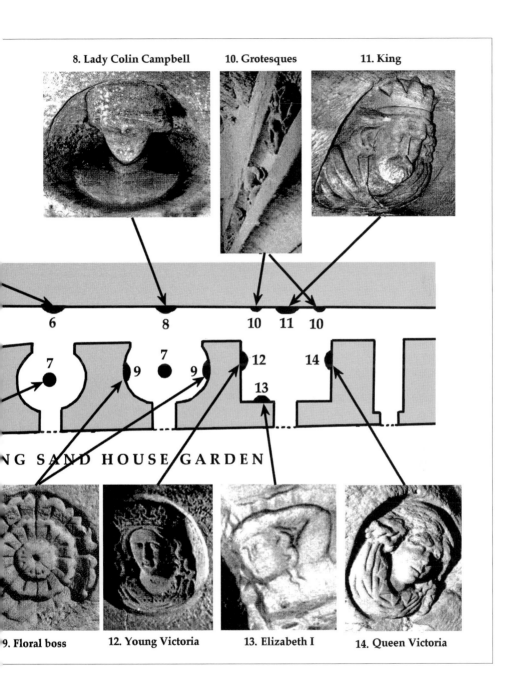

8. Lady Colin Campbell

10. Grotesques

11. King

6   8   10   11   10

7   9   7   9   12   14   13

NG SAND HOUSE GARDEN

9. Floral boss

12. Young Victoria

13. Elizabeth I

14. Queen Victoria

Fig. 3.4 The Cloisters, looking south.

Fig. 3.5 The Cherub.

was supposedly modelled on the subterranean cemeteries around Rome, the *Doncaster Gazette* of 2 August 1912 quoting:

> From the stable a sloping passage led down to a sort of crypt, a ghostly kind of place that Mr Senior is said to have modelled on the Catacombs at Rome.

We now turn south and climb a steady slope to approach the Cloisters. A detailed plan of this area is shown in Fig. 3.3.

The main passage is over 2 m (6 feet) wide and between 3 m (10 feet) and 4m (13 feet) high. The sunlight streams in through the windows to the right, illuminating almost 50 m (160 feet) of the arched tunnel (Fig. 3.4). As we reach the first adit, on our right, we look up to our left and there, high on the wall, we see the carved head and shoulders of a Cherub. He bears a crown from which flowers or leaves issue, and his feathered wings are spread behind him (Fig. 3.5).

Opposite the Cherub, at the far end of the adit, we see the first of eight windows and to the right of this stands the 2.9 m (9 feet 6 inches) tall figure of an Irishwoman in national costume. She is known as Molly, or Biddy (Fig. 3.6). Standing close by her, to the left of the window, is her awesome partner Pat, the Irishman. He holds a clay pipe in one hand and carries a shillelagh in the other. His mighty frame stands 3.5 m (11 feet 6 inches) tall (Fig. 3.7). Unfortunately, it is not known whether Biddy and Pat were modelled on particular characters, either real or mythical. However, it is possible that Biddy was, in fact, Biddy Early (1798–1874, baptised Bridget Ellen Connors), a well-known purveyor of herbal cures in the west of Ireland. Her first husband was named Pat Malley, giving further support to this theory.

Fig. 3.6 'Molly' or 'Biddy', the Irishwoman.

Fig. 3.7 'Pat' the Irishman.

Fig. 3.8 The Clown.

Fig. 3.9 The Elephant and Mahout.

Fig. 3.10 Pope and frieze beneath.

Fig. 3.11 Floral boss.

Proceeding 2 m (6 feet) along the tunnel the left-hand wall steps back slightly and in the corner thus formed is the bust of a Clown (Fig. 3.8). Opposite this figure, on the right, is perhaps the most memorable of all the carvings. This is the 3 m (10 foot) high form of an Elephant and its Mahout (Driver). The figures have been cleverly incorporated into a large roof-support column dividing the main tunnel from a short parallel passage connecting the first and second adits (Fig. 3.9).

There are no more notable carvings until we see the bust of a Pope opposite the fifth adit. Below the Pope is a section of deeply sculptured frieze (Fig. 3.10). The fifth and sixth adits have been formed into circular chambers and their domed ceilings and walls are adorned with floral bosses, of which Fig. 3.11 is a typical example.

Facing the sixth window is the carved head of a woman, referred to as Lady Colin Campbell. Born Gertrude Elizabeth Blood in May 1857, she enjoyed a liberal upbringing for the day and developed into an intelligent, artistic and beautiful young woman. She met Lord Colin Campbell MP in 1880 and became engaged to him three days later; they married the following year. Lady Colin Campbell moved in the highest social circles for several years, until the failure of her marriage led to the longest divorce case in English legal history.

To the window's left is the head of John Collier, alias Tim Bobbin, the eighteenth century Lancastrian author and painter. John Collier (18 December 1708–14 July 1786) was a caricaturist and satirical poet. He was born at Urmston, the son of an

Fig. 3.12 King.

Fig. 3.13 Queen Victoria in maturity.

Fig. 3.14 The Cloisters, looking north.

Fig. 3.15 Queen Victoria in her youth.

impoverished curate. Marriage and nine children meant he needed to supplement his income, thus he began producing illustrated satirical poetry in Lancashire dialect and a book of dialect terms. Much of his work was done in Rochdale and it was there that he died. It is said that he wrote his own epitaph twenty minutes before his death.

The penultimate adit is a large square chamber. The crowned head of a King (possibly Alfred) stares down from the left-hand wall of the main passage (Fig. 3.12). As we turn to face the window, on our left is Her Majesty Queen Victoria (Fig. 3.13), while alongside the window a much earlier sovereign, Queen Elizabeth I, adorns the wall.

Having walked a few more paces along the Cloisters and found no more carvings, we turn to look back in the direction we have travelled (Fig. 3.14). We now notice that the far wall of the penultimate chamber bears the bust of a young Queen Victoria (Fig. 3.15) opposite the effigy of her more mature self. Also evident are a number of grotesque heads carved below the King.

Not relishing the prospect of a walk into the darkness of the passage beneath the cemetery, we wander back towards the Catacombs, reflecting upon the strange collection of carvings and recalling some quotes about them and their possible creators.

The *Doncaster Review* of August 1894 suggests Henry had artistic inclinations himself:

In Mr. Senior's younger days much of his time was spent in oil painting, and there are many examples of his skill in the "Castle" [Sand House]. He has also a large collection of pictures by the old masters, many of them being very valuable. Indeed, the house is full of pictures and articles of virtu.

Expert on Victorian sculpture Terry Friedman, from Leeds Art Gallery, was asked for his comments about the Sand House and carvings in July 1987. He agreed there was no consistent theme to the carvings, and said that they showed 'a certain egocentricity.' They were merely the choice of an individual. There was some indication of imperial pride, i.e. Victoria, with the Elephant and Mahout suggesting an Indian connection. Terry asked if either William or Henry Senior had travelled to India, but there is no evidence to confirm this – an image of an Elephant and Mahout may have been seen by Henry in a book. Terry pointed out that the Cherub, grotesques, floral ornaments and ceiling bosses have an ecclesiastic look, maybe suggesting the sculptors' involvement with work on the rebuilding of the Doncaster Parish Church. In fact Terry thought they would be better described as master masons. They were probably artisans, but nevertheless good. The names of Thomas Scriven and Herring, who are mentioned as having associations with the Sand House, were not familiar as mainstream sculptors/ carvers to Terry, who added that the carvings beneath No. 69 Victoria Street were crude but interesting. Terry's comment in general on the carvings concluded that they were 'pure folk art of the very best.'

The name of Scriven is mentioned in several references relating to the carvings. In one article, 'Memories of the Unique Sand House,' *Don. Chron.* 1 January 1953, the following information appears:

> One of the men who carved in the Sand House was Mr. Tom Scriven, who had worked on the Doncaster Parish Church when it was rebuilt after the great fire of 1853. It is believed he moved straight from the church to assist Mr. Senior with his Sand House project.

It is true that Scriven worked as foreman to a Mr Philip, who was contracted to carry out carving work on St George's Parish Church when it was rebuilt after the fire. Scriven also resided in Doncaster for a while. But other than in newspaper articles which appeared after Henry's death, there is no firm evidence to link Tom Scriven's name to the Sand House.

A further link between St George's Church and the Sand House was attempted in a *Don. Gaz.* article dated 11 June 1936, illustrated with a picture (Fig. 3.16) and titled 'From Church to Sand House':

> ...the late Mr. Senior, with his assistants, exercised quite a measure of artistic taste in fashioning arches and pillars in the Gothic style out of the [sand] material. The carving shown in the illustration, however ... is not one of these products of "Sandy Senior's" own hand; the pillars and arches are of marble or other hard stone, and they appear to have been brought to the Sand House and built into the position they occupy there.

What is this? See Here and There note, "From Church to Sand House."

Fig. 3.16 Seat thought to have links with St George's Church.

I am told, but at present lack confirmation of the statement, that this particular feature of Sand House was brought from the old Doncaster Parish Church after the fire.

Other references suggest there was someone else involved, maybe working alone or with Scriven. In Henry Senior's obituary in the *Don. Chron.* 6 April 1900, it is said:

> In the solid rock of the passages are cut numerous figures, the work of a Mr Herring (not the painter need we say), and there are several pictures in the place painted by Mr Senior himself.

J. F. W. Lyons, in his article 'Castle of Sand was in Quarry', *Don. Gaz.* 29 June 1961, offers the following information, suppositions and whimsy:

> There were floral friezes running the length of the aisles, emblems and posies ornating the columns and domes, and on every side figures of kings, queens, and angel children executed in exquisite taste and skill.
>
> Off-setting these beautiful creations, suggesting the artist may have been indulging in a "lark" following a "binge" were many grotesque nightmarish figures of clowns, cherubs, bishops, gargoyles, reptiles and animals of all kinds.
>
> Sandy Senior is usually credited with having done all this work. But I was once told by a local man who claimed his father was personally acquainted with Senior, and

Fig. 3.17 The Cloisters, looking south.

had first-hand knowledge of the "castle," that all the sculptures were the work of two Italian masons who at the time were employed on rebuilding the Parish Church. To me, it seems the most probable story.

Despite the uncertainty, it cannot be denied that that the carvings had merit as agreed by the *Don. Gaz.* of 2 August 1912:

It should be mentioned that Mr. Senior employed the services of professional sculptors in beautifying his unique abode, and the figure mentioned [Diana, or 'Summer', in the gable entrance] bears the stamp of an artist whose skill was more than mediocre.

The *Don. Gaz.* of 2 August 1912 also commented on the condition of the carvings at that time:

Considering the nature of the material in which they are fashioned, and the many years that have elapsed since the sculptor's tool was used upon them, these figures and the other carvings in the corridor are wonderfully well-preserved, the very laces in Pat's boots being still distinguishable ... Catholicity is the watchword in the sculptural decoration of this wonderful passage, for the carver's art has been employed on such diverse subjects as a clown, a King and Queen of England, a Pope of Rome ... Then there are minor decorations, such as a horrific-looking vampire, sundry grotesques in the ecclesiastical genre, rose ornaments, and ceiling bosses from which. in Mr. Senior's days, gasoliers used to depend – for the creator of this store house of wonders had the place lighted by gas. There are some places in which the pillars have been rough hewn ready for other figures to be cut, but these have not been supplied. The striking feature about the place is the good state of preservation which the sculptures exhibit.

A comment on the price paid for the carvings comes from Horace Lumby, who lived at the Sand House with his family from 1900 to 1917. He told the *Don. Chron.* of 1 January 1953:

> [Mr] Senior ... employed two men at the then princely wages of 2s 6d per hour to cut carvings into the sandstone walls of the house and other buildings. The actual work of excavation was carried out by workmen employed by Mr. Senior.

Unfortunately, none of the preceding information was ever revealed in newspapers or other references during either William's or Henry's life time. Were the sculptures or carvings executed by Henry himself and his sons, Tom Scriven, a chap called Herring, two shadowy Italians or other artisans for *2s 6d* per hour? Frustratingly, we may never know the answer unless a major piece of information is unearthed in future years.

Putting those suppositions out of our head we have now returned to the Catacombs, but instead of leaving via the stable, we take the alternative route up a narrow flight of steps, pausing momentarily before we do so to glance back at the Cloisters (Fig. 3.17). The steps lead into a small summer house in the garden's north-east corner from whence we return not only to the brightness of the outside world but also to the year of 1900, where the Sand House narrative is resumed.

Chapter Four

The Sand House
in Corporation Ownership

A PICTURE of part of the Sand House, taken just before it was
destroyed.

Fig. 4.1 Possibly the last photograph taken of the Sand House.

THE SAND HOUSE IN CORPORATION OWNERSHIP

Following the sale of the Sand House to Doncaster Corporation, it soon became quite evident that there was no intention of dedicating the area for public leisure, since the entire complex was allocated for use by the Sanitary and Cleansing Department. The Corporation installed the Sanitary Department foreman, John Otter Lumby, and his family in the Sand House, the large premises allowing the spare rooms to be used for storage of Corporation equipment. Horse-drawn carts, used for night-soil and refuse collection, were kept in the open-fronted sheds to the rear of the house. Despite this apparent misuse of the area, there is evidence which suggests that social functions continued to be held there during the first decade of public ownership. Dances were reputedly one of the main attractions, with St James' Church Band, under the leadership of David Cameron, providing musical accompaniment. The house was also the venue for a happy event in 1909, when one of John Lumby's sons, Jabez Samuel, held his wedding reception there.

Probably the most detailed newspaper article ever written about the Sand House, at least while it remained in existence, was one previously referred to, which appeared in the *Don. Gaz.* of 2 August 1912. Not only did it provide a valuable description of the house and tunnels, but it was also illustrated by the first two photographs ever published of the area. These photographs, taken by H. L. Heaviside of Cleveland Street, belong to a set of at least twenty picture postcards for public sale, showing many house and tunnel views. They form the most comprehensive pictorial record ever produced of the Sand House. One of these cards, showing the Sand House viewed from Green Dyke Lane, is reproduced as Fig. 4.2. The 1912 article contains the first located reference to Henry Senior being nicknamed 'Sandy' by his contemporaries. In recent decades the pseudonym has been used almost to the exclusion of his real Christian name.

Evidence of the Sand House being open for public inspection is provided by the transfer of a ticket box from the Race Course to the house in December 1916. This was presumably to provide admission tickets for people wishing to view the property.

Horace Lumby, son of John, who lived at the Sand House with his mother and father from 1900 to 1917, gave a unique account of life in the property to a *Don. Chron.* reporter on 1 January 1953:

Fig. 4.2 The Sand House seen from Green Dyke Lane *c*. 1912.

It was plastered throughout, and although the floor of the living room was concrete there were wooden floors in many of the other rooms ... It was cosy and warm in winter, but in summer the contrast between the sunshine outside and the cool conditions indoors was very striking, and we had to have a fire throughout the year.

Horace recalled that visitors came from as far afield as Salt Lake City in the USA to see the Sand House, and added:

There was not what you could call a steady stream of visitors, but many people seemed interested and we were always pleased to show them round.

Answering a question about the size of the house he replied:

We were quite a large family. There were my mother and father, four boys and three sisters, and we had plenty of room. Four bedrooms and a bathroom formed the top storey and there was a similar number of rooms downstairs ... The garden in front of the house, originally the quarry floor, was very ornate and took some looking after. There were many fruit trees, mostly pears ... We used to have our letters delivered down a wooden chute from Albert Street, which was well above the roof level of the Sand House ... The bottom of the quarry was a pleasing well-cropped and tended garden occasionally used by the local branch of the British Women's Temperance Association for meetings and garden parties. [My mother] was a member of the branch.

Fig. 4.3 Hague family *c.* 1918.

John Otter Lumby was allegedly dismissed in 1917 as a result of an incident where the night-soil gang failed to dispose of the soil correctly and he hadn't known of their failure to do so. He was replaced by Thomas Hague, who subsequently moved into the Sand House with his wife and family. The Hague family can be seen in Fig. 4.3, with a view of the Sand House Long Room during their occupancy in Fig. 4.4. The latter photograph is taken from a second set of picture postcards, produced by William James Green in the 1920s.

William Green (26 April 1897–19 December 1973) operated his photography business from a studio in Doncaster's King's Arcade before giving up the profession in the late 1920s due to business being poor. Seen in Fig. 4.5, he subsequently became a travelling salesman and, later, a factory worker.

Heaviside and Green did a good photographic job in recording the Sand House and we shall be eternally grateful to them for their work. But without wishing to do them a disservice, they are virtually unknowns among Doncaster's giants of photography at that period. Very few photographers were operational in Doncaster during the early years of the art and so we may have missed out in having a photographic record during Henry Senior's time, which was the heyday of the Sand House. There are the two pictures of the two men, one allegedly Henry Senior himself, posing around the Sand House. These were printed from copy glass plate negatives and, if they do depict Henry, they are among the earliest pictures of him and indeed the Sand House. It is suspected that the copy negatives were taken by Luke Bagshaw, operating in Doncaster from the early 1890s until the 1930s. He was regarded as the godfather of photography in Doncaster, being Doncaster Corporation's official photographer for all their street widenings and other civic achievements and events. He was a photographic dealer and

Above: Fig. 4.4 The Long Room *c.* 1920.

Right: Fig. 4.5 William James Green, photographer.

also took countless photographs for other commercial operators, including brewers, colliery companies, architects and shop keepers. But he took nothing of the Sand House, a fact made even more puzzling when we know that his business premises were at 150-152 St Sepulchre Gate, a mere stone's throw from the Sand House. Then we move on to the commercial postcard people, including the likes of Edgar Leonard Scrivens, a giant amongst postcard photographers, not only in the South Yorkshire area, but in North Nottinghamshire and Derbyshire too. Scrivens documented virtually every event that occurred in Doncaster and fifty miles around, from colliery sinkings to new street layouts in colliery villages and from railway stations to royal visits. So why did he not photograph the Sand House? It is so frustrating not knowing the answer. His

Fig. 4.6 Shikell employee and horse with Victoria Street in background.

contemporaries, who included the Jameson brothers, the Roelichs, and others, never pointed their cameras at the Sand House either. Heaviside and Green have no great body of work like these other people and, as has been previously stated, are relatively unknown amongst Doncaster's photographers or producers of postcards. So let it be said again, we are grateful to them both, and for the occasional family snap of the Sand House.

During the First World War the army used the tunnels for ammunition storage and the house was permanently guarded by soldiers stationed at the front and rear. Also at that time, prior to the Hagues' arrival, a certain amount of unauthorised rubble and rubbish tipping had occurred at the sunken garden's Green Dyke Lane end. This had already obscured one or two of the Cloister windows. Thomas Hague, however, succeeded in preventing further tipping during his occupancy.

In 1919 a number of improvements were made to the Sand House in order to provide more modern living conditions. They included the relocation of the bath into what had been a bedroom, together with the provision of a hot water supply to the bath and kitchen. Furthermore, various structural repairs and redecoration were carried out, indicating a commitment by the Corporation to the long-term future of the premises and a wish to revive public interest in the place. However, the 1919 improvements were the last to be carried out.

Walter Shikell owned the company that supplied horses and horsemen to haul the refuse carts and night-soil carts for Doncaster Corporation, when the Sanitary Department was based at the Sand House. Walter owned all the horses and employed all the horsemen, but Doncaster Corporation owned most of the carts. Walter's son

Fig. 4.7 Arthur Shikell posing at rear of Sand House.

Arthur worked for the company and his grandson, also called Walter, had three interesting pictures of his grandfather's business operations in the Sand House area. Fig. 4.6 shows a man and a horse on the grassy area at the rear of the Sand House. Walter Shikell (the younger) thought the man was a former hansom cab driver from London, who worked for his grandfather. The carts in the photograph probably belonged to Doncaster Corporation. The wall in the background separated the Sand House property from the rear yards of Victoria Street, whose houses can be seen. Out of view to the left, the wall ended and there was an opening that led down a lane towards St Sepulchre Gate and the Alma Inn.

Fig. 4.7 portrays Arthur Shikell and a horse on the grassy area at the rear of the Sand House. In the centre background is the window of the office, which projected out from the back of the house. To the right is the Long Room's bay window and a bedroom window, above. At the far right is the path that led to the front of the house. To the left is a wide arched doorway giving access into the stable. This doorway was approached down a few long, shallow steps, suitable for horses. However, it is not thought that any horses were stabled there during the Corporation's ownership of the Sand House. The stable doorway was opposite the doorway in the front of the house, which was flanked by busts of Henry and Mary Senior.

Fig. 4.8 depicts horsemen and horses employed by Walter Shikell (the elder) to haul refuse and night-soil carts. The photograph is taken looking northwards and in the 'outer yard' area, between the rear yard of the Sand House and the narrow 'sand pit lane' leading to St Sepulchre Gate. Interested onlookers may be seen at the left and right of the photo. On the left are the rear elevations of houses and warehouses that

Fig. 4.8 Shikell horsemen and horses; St Sepulchre Gate is in the distance.

faced on to Albert Street (the houses had no rear doors). The long, narrow, curving block of buildings in the centre background is bounded by 'sand pit lane' on the left and the remaining section of Burden Lane on the right. At the far end of the block was the Alma Inn. Some of the buildings were stables. To the right of Burden Lane can be seen the houses of Victoria Place – some back-to-back houses lying between Burden Lane and Victoria Street.

By 1930 horse-drawn transport was becoming redundant and the Corporation, in response to this, introduced motorised refuse vehicles and accommodated them in a number of garages that were built at the rear of the Sand House. The widespread provision of water closets for the local houses also meant that night-soil collection had become unnecessary, further affecting the Corporation's use of the premises.

Thomas Hague's son, also called Thomas, lived in the Sand House from 1917 to 1932 and made the following points about the house, its garden, and the tunnels when talking to Richard Bell on 24 May 1983:

I still have a foot stool, one of a pair that we used to rest our feet on when sitting in the recessed seats by the kitchen window, as they were so high. Those in the other rooms were at a comfortable height. The stools were made from ship's timber by my grandfather, who was a shipwright. There were built-in cupboards in many of the rooms (corner cupboards and others).

All the downstairs ceilings were painted, but never re-decorated while we were there. The kitchen ceiling was whitewashed, with cornice round the edges.

Fig. 4.9 Sand House's front elevation, with Victoria Street above.

The roof was of pantiles on timber rafters and the ridge of the roof was approximately level with Green Dyke Lane. The tops of the upper windows were roughly level with Albert Street.

He went on to explain:

Before we moved in, about a quarter of the front garden was filled with tipped rubbish. A tennis court of about full size was later made on one of the lawns by my family and a grapevine grew along the cutting slope where the Cloisters windows looked out. There was a huge rhubarb patch, and twelve sticks were sold for a penny. The scene was very rural and quiet in the garden.

Fig. 4.10 Wheatley Senior School girls inspect the Sand House, 30 July 1936.

In relation to the tunnels he commented:

At the very end of the tunnel under the cemetery there was a hook on the wall where we used to hang lanterns. Without a lantern at the end of the tunnel it was absolutely dark. There were no gas lights in the tunnel during our occupation. I believe the carvings were done by Thomas Scriven.

G. R. Storry, in the *Yorkshire Evening Post* of 17 December 1963, added another First World War tale:

I must have been about sixteen when I first discovered the existence of this remarkable but strangely neglected curiosity ... I well remember Mr Hague's family. Mrs Hague grew so accustomed to our visits – we were constantly introducing friends to the Sand House and tunnels – that finally we were allowed to explore the tunnels without a guide. The most striking of the sandstone effigies in the tunnels were undoubtedly those of "Pat and Biddy, the Irish Giants" ... Poor "Biddy" had her nose sliced off by a bored sentry in World War I, when ammunition was stored in the main tunnel and Catacombs.'

Following the death of Thomas Hague in 1932, his widow and children had to leave the Sand House, their home for the previous fifteen years.

The next Sanitary Department foreman was a Mr Briggs, but he only occupied the premises for approximately two years, as by the mid-1930s the accommodation was becoming unsuitable for habitation, due to dampness and the general lack of modern conveniences. The Corporation's requirements were also changing, making the Sand House increasingly unsatisfactory for their purposes. A general idea of the condition of the house at this time may be gleaned from Figs 4.9 and 4.10.

On 21 November 1934, the Town Council's Estates Sub-committee decided that the house and tunnels should be boarded up. Action was delayed for a short time while a proposal to transfer responsibility for the Sand House was considered. At a Parks Committee meeting on 5 March 1935, the following motion was passed:

> The Sub-Committee considered the recommendation of the Estates Committee with respect to the taking over by the Parks Committee of the maintenance of the house, galleries and land at Sand House, other than the portion occupied by the Public Health Committee and it was resolved to recommend that the Estates Committee be thanked for their offer, but in view of the cost which would be incurred in restoring the premises to a reasonable state of repair they be informed that this Committee are unable to accept same. It was further recommended that if the Estates Committee will undertake the filling up of the land this committee will be prepared to maintain it as an open space.

The Committee thus totally disregarded the house as a place of immense public interest and merely agreed to maintain the area once it was filled in. This can only be construed as an act of gross irresponsibility by the Parks Committee.

On 13 March 1935 the Borough Surveyor was instructed to arrange for the site to be used as a tip, filling-in the house as well as the grounds. Also around this time a wall was built across the tunnel adjacent to the Elephant, to prevent access to the Cloisters. Furthermore, the house's roof was removed to allow the property to be backfilled, but neither the precise date of its removal, nor a reference to the demolition of any remaining structure, have been found.

Horace Lumby claimed:

> The last time I saw the Sand House was in 1938 when the Corporation were using the site as a tip. The roof had been ripped off and the place was a real mess.

The various Committee minutes are inconclusive, but tipping continued at the site for approximately ten years. Indeed, when a huge fire destroyed Woolworth's store in Doncaster town centre in May 1938, the debris from the site clearance, including damaged stock, was tipped at the Sand House site.

A further proposal for the area to be taken over by the Parks and Cemeteries Committee was considered in March 1946 but this was again rejected. By this time the area had been filled almost up to the original nineteenth century ground level, virtually obliterating all traces of the Sand House and sealing off access to the tunnels.

Fig. 4.11 shows an aerial view of the site, taken in 1951. Two years later, a foretaste of what was to come in subsequent years hit the front page of the *Don. Chron.* of 20 August 1953 in an article headed 'Subsidence Threat to Street':

Fig. 4.11 Aerial view taken in June 1951.

Fig. 4.12 Subsidence damage to Victoria Street house, 20 August 1953.

Large cracks have appeared in the walls of the houses overnight and one woman said she lay awake at night listening to "furniture moving about and walls creaking and groaning." Doncaster Borough Police are supervising nightly evacuations of the houses and Victoria Street is being specially patrolled. Preparations have been made at the Boy Scout headquarters opposite to accommodate families in case of emergency. The Chronicle understands that the houses, which are about 70 years old, are built near the site of a former sand quarry and it is suspected that the subsidence has been caused by the partial collapse of a tunnel under the houses ... Although the whole block has been affected, the worst hit are a group of five houses at the top. [O]ne of them [is] occupied by Mr. Walter Wildsmith ... [who] showed a Chronicle reporter into his cellar where there were large cracks, including one which leads into the next-door neighbour's home. The floor is tilted and twisted and there are indications of great strain and stress over the door jamb. [The picture which appeared with the article is reproduced as Fig. 4.12].

The effects of subsidence and the problems posed by the underground workings will be fully examined in Chapter 6 'Echoes from the Past'.

Chapter 5

The Hemingways
and No. 69 Victoria Street

Fig. 5.1 Portrait of William Hemingway, *c.* 1915.

THE HEMINGWAYS AND No. 69 VICTORIA STREET

Again it is necessary to digress from the main theme, on this occasion to study the Hemingway family's role in the Sand House area's development.

After marrying Henry Senior's daughter, William Hemingway became a foreman in the sand business. In 1878 he built two houses in Victoria Street, Nos 69 and 71, situated only 50 m (160 feet) from the Sand House. Apart from spending some time living at No. 32 Victoria Street, which he also owned, William and his wife Emma lived all their married life in No. 69, raising their family of eleven children.

William's part in running the business gradually became more important until, upon Henry's death, he took complete control. Fig. 5.2 shows a blank invoice from this period. According to a note on the reverse of the photograph, Fig. 5.3 portrays William Hemingway at the Sand House in August 1900, four months after Henry's death. He is standing next to a bust, reputedly of his recently-deceased father-in-law.

After the sand quarry had been fully exploited, sand was extracted from various underground excavations to the north of the Catacombs. The largest and most important of these was a cavern situated below the rear yards of Nos 69 and 71 Victoria Street. This cavern ultimately measured approximately 20 m (65 feet) by 7 m (23 feet) and its vaulted roof was over 4 m (13 feet) high. Access to the cavern was via two flights of steep, narrow steps leading down from No. 69's cellar. Fig. 5.4 depicts the bottom steps leading into the cavern. As previously mentioned, there was also a tunnel connecting this cavern to the Sand House workings, but at some stage this was sealed off. Furthermore, a vertical shaft in the rear yard of No. 69 allowed sand to be winched up from below, although later this shaft was used to tip building rubble down into the cavern.

The cavern's excavation date is unknown, but it is likely that it was commenced soon after William Hemingway built the houses. It gradually developed as sand was extracted for sale, and reached its full extent by the First World War. As sections of the cavern were completed, they were decorated with carvings worked on by several Hemingway family members, as indicated by the variable quality of the results. Most of these took the form of human figures, as shown in Figs 5.5, 5.6, 5.7 and

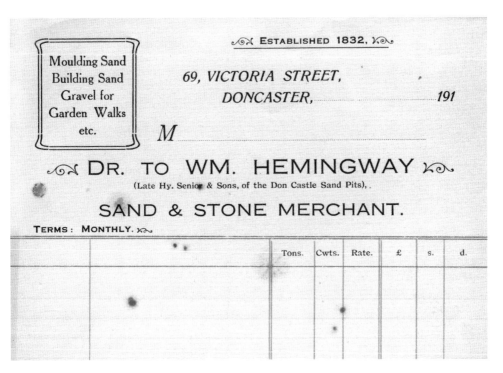

Fig. 5.2 Blank invoice.

Fig. 5.3 William Hemingway, August 1900.

Fig. 5.4 Steps entering the cavern from the cellar of No. 69 Victoria Street.

5.8. They were mainly created by William's sons – George, a bricklayer and Edgar, a stonemason; both emigrated to Australia in 1912. William and another son were also reputed to have had a hand in the carving work. In addition to the human figures, other items carved included plaques to commemorate the reigns of Queen Victoria and King Edward VII.

After Emma Hemingway died in 1907, William eventually remarried and continued to live at No. 69 until his own death in 1919. Even then the house remained in family ownership and its final occupants, before demolition in 1968, were William's youngest son, Joseph Cyril Hemingway, and his family. No. 69 Victoria Street is pictured in Fig. 5.9, just prior to its demolition, when quite a drama occurred. The *Doncaster Evening Post* of 21 December 1967 reported:

More tunnels with carvings on the walls, near the Balby Bridge site where a £1 million housing scheme is under way, are being investigated by Doncaster Corporation officials. Extensive investigations were being made before work began on the scheme, which is to include a 16-storey block of flats; and the tunnels constructed by 19th Century sand merchant [Henry] Senior were [being] plotted by experts. The discovery of yet another tunnel, or cavern, will not affect the current development, but it could affect the lay-out of the second stage. Workmen employed by Middleton's, the Sprotbrough demolition contractors, who were preparing to demolish a house in Victoria Street, found that a cellar led down into an arch-shaped cavern, with life-sized figures carved into the walls. "We got most of the caverns plotted before we could start the first phase of the development," said the Borough Architect, Mr L. J. Tucker. "But we shall have to investigate this one, which we didn't know anything about, before we can plan the next stage. We have not yet determined the lay-out of the second phase, but we shall obviously not have to put anything substantial over this cavern."

But if the cavern was unknown to the Corporation it was certainly not unknown to 71-year-old Joseph Cyril Hemingway, who lived in the house above it ... "I have tried to tell them about it before, but nobody seemed interested ... My grandfather [Henry Senior] and his men used to get the sand out and send it by rail to various places, particularly Barnsley, to Qualter Hall's. It was not building sand. It was moulding sand ... There used to be a tunnel which went under Victoria Street, linking the workings at our side with the workings on the other side. There were also three big arches, which were bricked up. In our garden there was a well about three feet [0.9 m] wide by two feet six [0.8 m], into the chamber below our garden and the garden next door.

They used buckets and a windlass to get the sand up. Two of my brothers, who are now in Australia, did the carvings in this cavern. George, who is 83, was a bricklayer, and Edgar, who is 79, was a stonemason ... They were very good at it and my father, Mr William Hemingway, also had a go at it. He made a figure of a woman about eight feet [2.4m] high. Edgar carved the figure of a woman wearing combinations.

He copied it from a newspaper advertisement of Dennis Roberts' who used to have a drapery shop in Doncaster." The two brothers also carved plaques commemorating

Fig. 5.5 Carving in cavern below No. 69 Victoria Street.

Fig. 5.6 Carving in cavern below No. 69 Victoria Street.

Fig. 5.7 Carving in cavern below No. 69 Victoria Street.

Fig. 5.8 Carving in cavern below No. 69 Victoria Street.

Queen Victoria and King Edward VII. Another brother – there were eight of them – carved a large cup and saucer, but he was obviously not as good an artist as George and Edgar. There was also a bust, set high in a niche in the wall, which is a bit of a puzzle.

"I am told it was supposed to be George III and I would have taken it out, but I couldn't get it. That is not carved into the wall. I think it [was] made of chalk."

Alan Berry, in the *Doncaster Star* of 7 September 1988, described the time when Electricity Board meter man, Raymond Stenson, went to No. 69 Victoria Street in 1967 to read and remove the meter and disconnect the power supply and, more importantly, what he found:

Number 69 was the only house left standing; all around it had been demolished, the place was becoming derelict and new houses and high-rise flats [were] being built nearby. Raymond descended into the cellar and did the job he had gone to do. In the pitch darkness that he had created, he used his torch to return to the surface, but just as he was turning into daylight he noticed a door. A door which, it seemed to him, could serve no useful purpose. Who could want a door directly into what ought to be earth? Pushing it open, and shining his torch he suddenly found himself descending steep narrow steps roughly-hewn into the hard sandstone. About 14 feet [4 m] below the surface the steps turned into a huge passage ... The stench was almost overpowering, but Raymond, having no idea what he had stumbled on, pressed on. Suddenly a huge face stared down at him from the roof. Then another and another. It was like a scene from a horror movie. And there was a curious plaque about Queen Victoria. Raymond would have gone on, but the smell, which he thought at first might be escaped gas, forced him back to the surface. On returning to daylight, astonished at what he had seen, he met a group of three little boys playing round the remains of Number 69. "Don't you go in there," said a rather shaken Raymond Stenson. "It's dangerous." At this very moment, unknown to him until the evening newspaper came out that night, he was being observed. A [*Don. E. Post*] photographer, illustrating a story about the demolitions and the new buildings that were replacing them, took a shot of him and the boys [see Fig. 5.9 once more].

Just before Christmas 1967 (as reported in *Don. E. Post*, 11 January 1968), the Doncaster Museum and Art Gallery staff abandoned an attempt to cut out and preserve sandstone carvings in the cellar of No. 69 Victoria Street:

"We had begun working on it but during our absence damage was done and we have had to abandon it," said J. R. Lidster, acting head of the museum.

"Someone went in and knocked pieces off them and they are not worth preserving now. We had started cutting one out with a mason's electric drill, but the head of it was knocked off. It is a big job and needed more time and more specialist equipment than we have to deal with it. It's a great disappointment, they were good examples of

Fig. 5.9 No. 69
Victoria Street,
December 1967.

folk art, but this is one of the risks you run when you are working in a town." [Fig.
5.10 precisely captures the conditions in the cavern beneath No. 69].

Harry Claxton was reported in 1968 as going down into the Sand House tunnels to
try and remove some carvings, after reading in the local press of unsuccessful attempts
by museum staff to do so. He referred to the carvings under No. 69 Victoria Street as
being of poor quality and, in fact, wasn't impressed by the quality of those in the main
tunnel. He thought it unlikely that the carvings in No. 69 were vandalised overnight,
as the newspaper reported, as he remembered a night watchman being on duty. He
borrowed the night watchman's lamp on one occasion to go into the tunnels during the
evening. Harry was unsuccessful in removing carvings as there was insufficient time
before the tunnels were sealed.

Fig. 5.10 Partially infilled cavern below No. 69 Victoria Street.

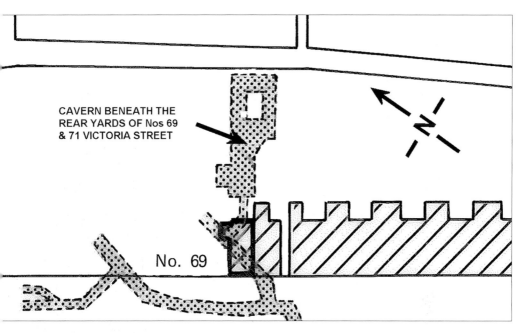

CAVERN BENEATH THE
REAR YARDS OF Nos 69
& 71 VICTORIA STREET

No. 69

Fig. 5.11 Extent and location of cavern beneath No. 69 Victoria Street.

With No. 69 Victoria Street vacated and soon demolished, so ended a direct link between the Senior/Hemingway family and this district of Doncaster, which stretched back for almost 140 years.

Even after No. 69's demolition, it continued to make its former presence felt. In 1970 there was an incident in what was becoming an increasingly unwelcome and expensive series of manifestations of the Victoria Street underground excavations. Arriving home from work one Sunday, Green Dyke Lane resident Maurice Dunston was alerted by some local children claiming that they had found 'the Sand 'Ole.' Knowing of the folklore of the mysterious tunnels of the area, Maurice followed the children to the now flattened Victoria Street, where they led him to a vertical shaft of approximately 1.5 m (5 feet) diameter, tapering down to a small square hole about 3 m (10 feet) below the surface. Below that there seemed to be a large void.

The children had found a pneumatic hose lying nearby and had tied it to the makeshift scaffolding barrier that someone had erected around the shaft.

Using the hose for support and with a bicycle lamp in hand, Maurice lowered himself down the shaft and through the square hole into the void beneath. Although he didn't know it at the time, he had entered the cavern formerly below the rear yards of Nos 69 and 71 Victoria Street, made temporarily accessible by the collapse of the fill material above the 'well' created by the Hemingways many decades earlier.

Maurice spent several minutes underground, amazed by the remains of the carved figures and plaques which appeared out of the gloom as the light from his bicycle lamp fell upon them. But as the children on the ground surface were being less than helpful by throwing stones down the shaft, and fearing for his safety should there be a further fall of material, he decided to retreat to the daylight above, his head filled with the curious images he had just witnessed.

Even though this unintended access route was re-sealed soon after Maurice Dunston's underground visit, the Victoria Street excavations were to make the headlines several more times, as we shall see in the next chapter. Fig. 5.11 indicates the extent and location of the cavern in relation to No. 69 Victoria Street.

Chapter 6
Echoes from
the Past

Fig. 6.1 Jeff. Hoggarth seen in the Cloisters, January 1976.

ECHOES FROM THE PAST

Although the Sand House was destroyed by the late 1940s (Fig. 4.11), the underground passages were still intact. In 1949, however, it was necessary to place 12 tonnes of backfill in a hole which appeared in the cellar of a house on Victoria Street's west side. It seems that the subsidence was caused by the partial collapse of one of Henry Senior's tunnels.

A similar, though more dramatic, incident was reported on the *Doncaster Chronicle*'s front page on 20 August 1953, as we detailed earlier.

After these two incidents, no mention of the Sand House has been located until 29 June 1961, when local historian J. F. W. Lyons wrote an article for the *Don. Gaz.* in which he gave a brief history of the area. He reflected that the Doncaster Corporation seemed to have made no attempt to preserve the house or exploit it commercially. The only area that remained was a vast expanse of scrub-grown, unused land and a rusted, broken iron gate, marking the former entrance from Green Dyke Lane. An accompanying photograph illustrated the desolation of the site (Fig. 6.2). A further photograph, taken from Victoria Street, reveals the northern section of the Sand House site, along with a remaining part of Albert Street and Elsworth Street beyond (Fig. 6.3).

From the early 1960s, a number of newspaper articles reported on the search for, or the rediscovery of, tunnels. This subsequently prompted readers to send in letters which reminisced about involvement with the house. Whilst this showed a welcome degree of interest by Doncaster people, it unfortunately gave rise to erroneous reports which perpetuated myths about the area. The persistent references to George Senior being the Sand House's creator were perhaps the most remarkable.

The 1960s were a time of extensive redevelopment in Doncaster, as in many other towns. Large expanses of Victorian terraced houses were cleared to make way for modern dwellings. Doncaster Corporation followed the 1960s trend for high-rise blocks of flats. A public inquiry into the compulsory purchase order being sought for the clearance of Albert Street and Victoria Street was held in Doncaster's Mansion House on 17 January 1962. It was proposed to acquire and demolish fifty properties, to enable flats to be built. The application was successful, but the Corporation realised

THE SITE of the quarry in which Sand Rock Castle was built. On the left of the picture is Albert Street, running into St. Sepulchre Gate. On the right (with St. James' Church spire in the background), is the Victoria Hall. The picture was taken from Green Dyke Lane, which runs alongside the Old Cemetery.

Fig. 6.2 Sand House site from Green Dyke Lane, June 1961.

that extensive investigations would be necessary to determine the locations of the underground tunnels before new construction could begin. Indeed, planning officials expressed serious doubts over the project's viability if costly foundation work had to be carried out.

The *Don. Chron.* of 25 April 1963 elaborated in 'Old Tunnels Problem for Today's Planners':

> A man who tunnelled a honeycomb of passageways under Doncaster in the 19th century caused a skyscraper-sized problem for the town's 20th century planners. It is feared that the tunnelling might have made the land unsafe for skyscraper tower blocks of flats proposed in the area and they might have to be scrapped. The land involved is bang in the middle of Doncaster's biggest redevelopment block where it was hoped that a fine new residential area would rise following a sweeping slum clearance. It is the area bounded by St James' Street, St Sepulchre Gate, St Swithin's Terrace and Green Dyke Lane. A Corporation Town Planning Official told the Chronicle "The tunnels could seriously jeopardise our plans for the area. The cost of filling-in and piling down could make it uneconomical to build tower blocks there." ... Today the entrance to the tunnel is buried under tons of dirt and rubble. "Filling in the tunnels would be a costly and specialised job" said the Town Planning official. "It would probably be necessary to pile down until a solid base was reached."

Reports of the Corporation's building proposals prompted Richard Storry, a Fellow of St Antony's College, Oxford, to write one of several letters to the local press recalling the Sand House and deploring its demise (*Yorks. E. Post* 17 December 1963). In his view:

> To have turned that green hollow into a refuse dump was an act of barbaric stupidity. To build high flats over the warren of the Catacombs would seem to be less barbaric but, perhaps, hardly less stupid.

Fig. 6.3 Section of Sand House site with Albert and Elsworth Streets beyond.

In late 1963 the Corporation commissioned a technical investigation of the area, which was undertaken by a Sheffield firm, Geotechnical and Concrete Services Ltd. The investigation's purpose was two-fold. Firstly, information was required to assist in designing foundations for blocks of dwellings up to fourteen storeys high. Therefore, particular reference had to be made to the material used for backfilling the former sand quarry. The second objective was to discover the extent of the tunnelling. Three different techniques were employed to obtain the required information. Initially, twenty-one boreholes were drilled at the site to measure the thickness of the strata and to take samples for testing purposes. The second technique took the form of an electrical resistivity survey. In this technique, variations in resistivity of particular areas of ground were measured and correlated against known variations in rock types and the presence of voids such as tunnels. The third method of investigation was employed because of inconclusive results from the resistivity survey. It involved making access into the tunnels and plotting their size and layout by a conventional theodolite survey.

The quest for more information regarding the layout of the tunnels led the *Don. Gaz.* to run a story on its front page of 7 May 1964 headed 'Digging out the house that "Sandy" built'. It revealed these details:

> The glories of Doncaster's famous Sand House, filled in years ago, are to be uncovered again – for a short time. Already, workmen have uncovered the mouth of a couple of caves ... The Borough Architect, Mr L. Tucker [said]: "We have made a survey of the caves and tunnels by surface boring. Now we intend actually going into the tunnels to find out where they go, whether they are filled in and what sort of structure the land

Fig. 6.4 Excavation for
tunnel survey,
May 1964.

would support." ... The present work at the site will uncover just how thoroughly the
quarry was filled in.

Excavation in the former quarry area commenced at the end of April 1964 and a
breakthrough into the tunnels was made on 6 May.
    The *Yorks. E. Post* of 8 May 1964 reported:

Following a survey this week on the site of the old Sand House at Green Dyke Lane,
Doncaster, there still remains a lot of speculation as to where some of the old tunnels,
carved in the rock, lead to. About 1,000 cu. yds of earth was removed to reveal the
entrance to the main tunnel, which was blocked off when the old sand quarry was filled
up ... The first thing that surveyors from Geotechnical and Concrete Services were
confronted with when they entered the tunnel was a bank of foul air. A Sheffield area
colliery manager was called in to test the air, but a through current quickly ventilated

the tunnel ... The main tunnel is the one that the surveyors are plotting in relation to the surface, but local rumours say that there are many other cavities in the area. It is not certain whether the old rock house was knocked down or just filled in with the debris that was taken to the site ... Others claim to have made their way through a network of tunnels which opened out on the sand-rock railway embankment beneath the Vine Hotel. But wherever the tunnels run to, nobody is likely to get into them, for when the surveyors complete their work ... the tons of earth that were moved to reveal the 19th century wonder will be pushed back into place – maybe to seal the cavity for ever.

Fig. 6.4 shows the excavation which gave access to the passages. Of the entrances illustrated, the one on the right was the northern-most window position, adjacent to which Pat and Biddy stood. To its left was the one that originally gave access from inside the summer-house. The surveyors found that the Catacombs had been partially backfilled, presumably during the period when tipping in the quarry was taking place. Part of the area is illustrated in Fig. 6.5. The headroom had been substantially reduced by filling and the material generally used for this purpose was sand. However, in the photograph large pieces of rubble can clearly be seen in the foreground.

Fig. 6.5 The Catacombs.

Fig. 6.6 Manhole under Green Dyke Lane.

A reminder of the 'sewerage tunnel's' origins was provided by a brick manhole located under Green Dyke Lane. Fig. 6.6 shows the 1.5 m (5 feet) square chamber, which was built to give access from the ground surface to the sewer running beneath the tunnel floor. The part of the tunnel with the smallest cross-sectional area was that below the cemetery. An impression of its size and shape can be gained from Fig. 6.7.

The surveyors determined that the original floor of the entire tunnel was roughly level and approximately 9 m (30 feet) below ground surface. The roof level varied considerably but, apart from one major fall under Green Dyke Lane, was in generally sound condition. It was estimated that some 1.5 m (5 feet) of solid rock was left above the tunnels, plus an overburden of sand, clay, bricks, rubble, ashes and gravel. A close examination of the excavations revealed that, except at the sides adjacent to the quarry and at the northern extremity, all walls were of solid sandstone. It was therefore concluded that the full extent of the eastern and southern boundaries of the original excavations had been determined (the reader may wish to refer to Fig. 2.21 to see the limits of the workings). Nevertheless the resistivity survey suggested the presence of other separate galleries, not connected to the main workings, and as many as four other excavations were suspected.

In conclusion, the technical report recommended that all located workings be completely filled and all foundations in the area be taken down to solid sandstone, or

Fig. 6.7 'Sewerage tunnel' below Hyde Park (Doncaster) Cemetery.

a depth of 9 m (30 feet), whichever was the greater. Firm evidence about the amount of filling carried out at this time has not been ascertained, but later it was revealed that any such work had been far from complete. The reason for such a crucial recommendation not being implemented is unknown.

Fig. 6.8 details the type of foundations generally used in ground conditions such as those encountered in the Victoria Street area. A grid of piles is constructed which carries the weight of the building superstructure down to a suitable load-bearing stratum, usually bed-rock. This avoids carrying any load on the suspect strata nearer the ground surface and prevents any possibility of subsidence resulting from the presence of voids or soft material under the building.

By the early 1970s, all the Victoria Street and adjacent streets' houses had been cleared and in their place stood a seventeen-storey-tall block of flats, Silverwood House, and many low-rise blocks. The street had lost its identity, becoming an extension of St James' Street. It also seemed that all traces of the Sand House and its tunnels had been finally obliterated. However, implementation of a major highway improvement scheme soon afforded new opportunities to inspect those tunnels which, for some reason, as mentioned earlier, had not been filled in. The Balby Bridge interchange scheme, carried out by A. F. Budge Ltd, involved widening Green Dyke Lane to become a continuation of the Carr House Road dual carriageway and the construction of a flyover and roundabout at its junction with Cleveland Street (formerly part of St Sepulchre Gate).

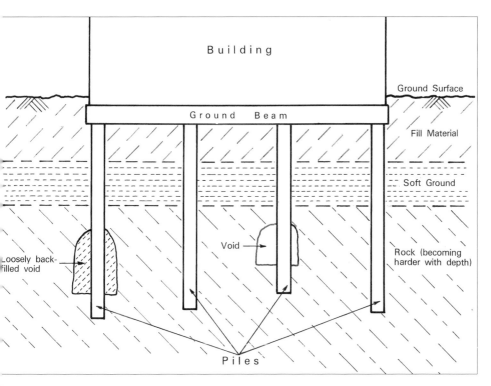

Fig. 6.8 Typical foundations for large structures in poor ground.

In January 1976, investigations took place and were detailed in the *Chartered Surveyor* of July 1976:

The physical condition of the tunnels was in doubt so in order to check the accuracy of the only existing plan and at the same time to obtain access to the tunnels in order to make an inspection it was decided to put down two large diameter boreholes [Figs 6.9 and 6.10] ... Two 3 feet [0.9 m] diameter boreholes were put down on to the line of the tunnels at approximately 70 feet [21 m] centres ... The first party down the hole was led by the District Inspector of Mines, accompanied by the Area Safety Officer of the National Coal Board. As might be expected, there was a good ventilation circuit between the boreholes: elsewhere air was stagnant but breathable. Despite a complete absence of roof supports, roof conditions were good and the tunnels appeared to be standing as well as when they were first driven. The only appreciable deterioration was in an area of heavy root penetration where tree roots had found their way through some 28 feet [9 m] of cover to cause flaking of the sandstone. The minimum depth of cover was recorded beneath a cemetery, just 16 feet [5 m]. This left only 10 feet [3 m] between the roof of the tunnel and the overlying graves – a macabre thought to those in the tunnels. From an engineering point of view the problem was now readily definable and could easily be dealt with. Although the tunnels were standing well, it was not thought desirable to leave such large cavities close to the surface

Above: Fig. 6.9 Borehole sunk in Green Dyke Lane, 1976.

Left: Fig. 6.10 Jeff Hoggarth descending into the Cloisters, 1976.

beneath a major highway and accordingly the decision was made to grout that part of tunnel beneath the line of the road. Barriers were constructed underground to isolate the length of tunnel to be treated and the void filled with a fly ash/cement mixture. The two main boreholes were utilised both for grouting and the transfer of materials underground with a number of small diameter holes being drilled to allow topping up of the grout to take place.

This opportunity to view the passages was taken by the South Yorkshire County Council archaeologist, John Little, and Doncaster Museum and Art Gallery's archaeological field officer, Paul Buckland. Consequently, a full set of photographs of the remaining passages was obtained.

Fig. 6.11 shows one of the decorated adits near the Cloisters' south end. The debris partially filling the chamber had spilled through the opening where a window had once overlooked the Sand House garden.

A general view northwards along the Cloisters is given in Fig. 6.12. John Little is seen examining the carved frieze near the badly eroded bust of the Pope. As mentioned earlier, when the tunnels were sealed off in the 1930s, a wall was built across the main passage, alongside the Elephant. The highway contractor's sub-agent, Jeff Hoggarth, is pictured in Fig. 6.13 standing by the wall, examining the Clown. Celebrated local journalist Stephen McClarence can be seen in the Cloisters in Fig. 6.14, in preparation

Fig. 6.11 A decorated adit in the Cloisters.

Fig. 6.12 John Little in the Cloisters, January 1976.

Fig. 6.13 Jeff Hoggarth examining the Clown.

for his article 'Engineers probe the Sand House' *Don. E. Post* 22 January 1976. Further examples of the condition of the carvings are given in Figs 6.15, 6.16 and 6.17.

As reported by *Chartered Surveyor*, the decision was made to fill-in the tunnel under the dual carriageway. A pulverised fuel ash (PFA) grout was pumped in, to seal that section. The highway improvements completed the area's transformation from its appearance in Henry Senior's day. See Fig. 6.18 for the present street layout in relation to the Sand House and tunnels.

Amazingly, but predictably perhaps, in the light of the in-filling being incomplete, further problems arose from the presence of underground passages in February 1982 and April 1983.

In one instance, an adjacent building suffered slight damage due to settlement. The *Don. E. Post* of 17 February 1982 elaborated in typically sensationalist fashion:

Fig. 6.14 Stephen McClarence in the Cloisters.

Fig. 6.15 Cloisters carvings in January 1976.

The collapse of a sewer in St James' Street has led to the rediscovery of a bit of Doncaster's history – one of the tunnels constructed in the late 19th century by [the Seniors]. It was after a council road-sweeping vehicle had sunk into the road – just eight feet [2.4 m] from the entrance to a subway – that the discovery was made.

Council workmen dug down to investigate the cause of the collapse and about 15 feet [4.6m] below the road surface found the roof of the tunnel and a further five feet [1.5m] down was the fractured sewer. The road has been closed and workmen are probing the extent of the tunnels to find out how best to seal them off. "When the road surface went down we wondered what on earth was happening" said Peter Greaves, the council's Director of Technical Services. "We have dug down now and found a surface water sewer, which was put in during the early 1950s, has collapsed where it crosses one of the small tunnels of the old Sand House area."

He thought the sewer had fractured, water had escaped, eroding the sand filling round it into the cavities of the tunnel and taking away the supports from the sewer, causing it to collapse.

The *Don. Star* of June 1983 detailed how the sewer collapse was to be tackled:

Doncaster Borough council have asked experts from Birmingham University to carry out radar tests in the honeycomb of caves in the St James' Street area ... Peter

Fig. 6.16 Cloisters carvings in January 1976.

Fig. 6.17 Cloisters carving in January 1976.

Greaves, the council's technical services director, said the work was being carried out as a precaution. "There is no need for people to panic. The homes in that area are very well built," he said. One house has already started to crack after the sewers collapsed but council officials say there are no other signs of damage from the sand workings. Mr. Greaves said when the initial probe was carried out just before the houses were built in 1963, they were hampered by gas. "Now this test will find out the extent of the workings and assess what work needs doing, if any, to stop further collapses. Damage to property so far has been caused by a sideways movement, after the sewer collapsed ... If it is necessary to carry out filling operations we shall then apply to the Department of the Environment for a grant to cover the cost of the works."

Expensive repairs to the sewers were undertaken, necessitating large excavations in St James' Street. This led Doncaster Metropolitan Borough Council to investigate the possibility of filling all the remaining voids, to prevent any future problems arising.

In the *Don. Star* of 13 December 1983 a council spokesman said:

The sands of time are running out. We are not saying this area is immediately dangerous, but it could become so over the next 30 years.

The *Don. Star* added:

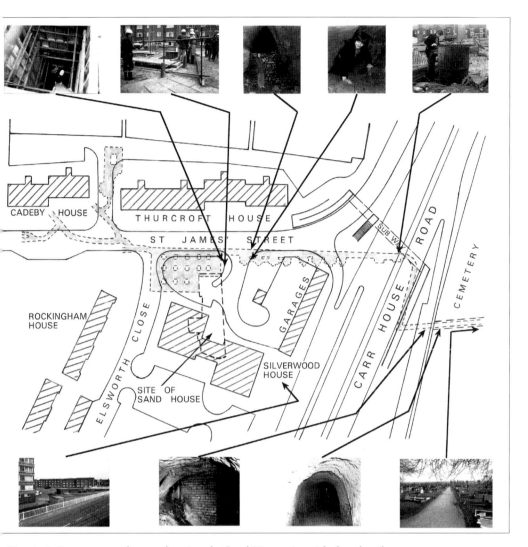

Fig. 6.18 Present street layout showing the Sand House site with thumbnails.

They still do not know the full extent of [the] Senior's underground galler[ies] ... so they will be probing to ensure that every inch is filled in ... The Government have agreed to give the council a 100 per cent grant to carry out the scheme, and if the operation costs more it will consider providing that as well. Workmen are expected to move in during January, pouring silos of pulverised ash from Thorpe Marsh power station into the holes.

A grant to finance the project was obtained from the Department of the Environment, enabling work to begin in February 1984. Fig. 6.19 shows the shaft sunk in Silverwood House car park to give access into the Catacombs and Cloisters.

On 16 February 1984 a group of Henry Senior's descendants, including Richard Bell, was allowed to enter the tunnels, under the supervision of staff from contractor

Fig. 6.19 Shaft access into Catacombs and Cloisters, February 1984.

Fig. 6.20 An employee of G. L. Quine with safety equipment in the Cloisters.

Fig. 6.21 Remains of the Elephant and Mahout, February 1984.

Fig. 6.22 The poor state of the Clown, February 1984.

G. L. Quine Ltd (Fig. 6.20). The Cloisters (extending as far as the dual carriageway) were accessible, as were some parts of the Catacombs, enabling many of the carvings to be photographed (Figs 6.21, 6.22 and 6.23). A few days later three people, David Mahoney, Patricia Henson and Derek Woolley, gained unauthorised access to the tunnels and dramatically staged a 'sit-in' for several hours to protest at the filling-in of the unique excavations. The *Don. Star* of 20 Feb 1984 elaborated:

> Protesters staged a sit-in today in a last-ditch attempt to save a unique slice of Doncaster's history. Two men and a woman spent four hours at the bottom of a sand tunnel 25 feet [8m] below the surface in a bid to win a reprieve for a Victorian eccentricity, the Sand House, created by [Henry/William] Senior. But they failed to convince Doncaster Council to think again and preserve it for posterity – and workmen were expected to begin filling in the tunnel ... The campaign leader ... David Mahoney ... said: "I am terribly upset about it going and think it is wrong." He was

Fig. 6.23 The King still in good condition, February 1984.

Fig. 6.24 Backfilled boreholes to the rear of Cadeby House.

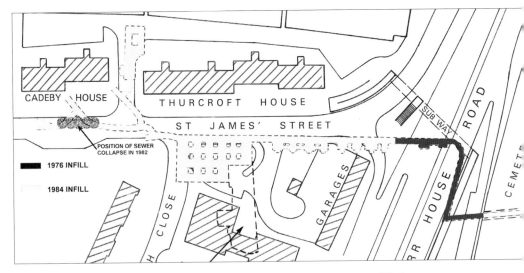

Fig. 6.25 Plan showing when various sections of the tunnels were infilled.

Fig. 6.26 Hyde Park (Doncaster) Cemetery over the line of remaining tunnel.

joined by Patricia Henson and Derek Woolley. [Doncaster Council] believes the site could prove dangerous if nearby sewers collapse. AND IT IS DETERMINED TO FILL THEM IN FOR GOOD.

David Mahoney was interviewed on Radio Hallam on the subject of the sit-in and stated that it was also mentioned on Yorkshire Television's news programme *Calendar*. However, the protest was abortive and a pulverised fuel ash grout was subsequently pumped into the passages to finally seal them.

G. L. Quine Ltd, carried out test drilling of the surrounding area (Fig. 6.24) in an attempt to locate any remaining voids and, with the help of information from Richard Bell, located the cavern formerly under No. 69 Victoria Street. As it revealed signs of structural deterioration, it was also grouted up. No other tunnels were located despite the extensive investigations.

This grant-aided project could have been expected to end the Sand House story completely, but this was not to be. A further sewer collapse occurred in St James' Street in October 1985 near to the site of No. 69 Victoria Street. Examination revealed a small tunnel heading north-eastwards towards Cadeby House, but, apart from a short length near the collapse, it had been back-filled with sand, presumably many years earlier. Nevertheless, further grouting was carried out, the sewer was reinstated, and another new rectangle of tarmacadam was added to the patchwork of St James' Street. Fig. 6.25 indicates when various sections of the tunnels were infilled. The only tunnel remaining unfilled lies beneath a path running south-eastwards in Hyde Park (Doncaster) Cemetery (Fig. 6.26).

At the time of writing (July 2010) no further evidence of Henry Senior's work has manifested itself, but experience suggests that Doncaster may not yet have seen the last of the Sand House tunnels.

Fig. 6.27 Looking southwards on the former line of Victoria Street, July 2010.

Left: Fig. 6.28 Looking northwards over the Sand House site, July 2010.

Below: Fig. 6.29 The Sand House superimposed on the present-day landscape.

Indeed, it is possible that one day, when Silverwood House and its neighbouring buildings have been cleared away, archaeologists may uncover the site and remove the grout, restoring the Cloisters and Catacombs to their former glory. Even part of the Sand House itself, buried for seventy years already, may once again be open for public inspection.

Today, looking southwards on the former line of Victoria Street (Fig. 6.27) and northwards over the Sand House site (Fig. 6.28), it is difficult to imagine the pleasant green hollow which existed a century ago, but we include Fig. 6.29, which superimposes the Sand House onto the present-day landscape.

The statements of the Estates Committee Chairman, in January 1935, that there was no intention of submerging the house, that the Committee wanted to preserve it for future generations, and that the gallery would not be interfered with at all, can now sadly be seen in their true perspective.

As the Sand House progressively fades from living memory, we reflect on what a truly exceptional contribution Henry Senior made to his home town of Doncaster. His life's work was neatly summarised in his obituary (*Don. Gaz.* 6 April 1900), extracts from which are reproduced as Figs 6.30 and 6.31.

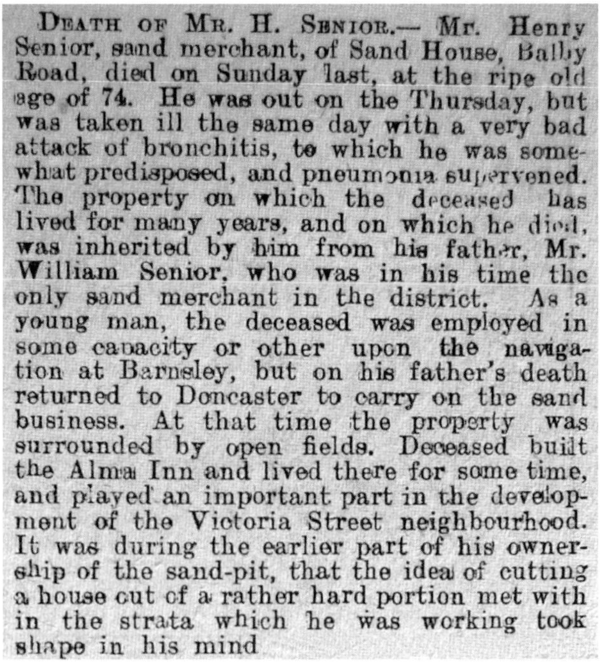

Fig. 6.30 Extract from Henry Senior's obituary, April 1900.

DEATH OF MR. H. SENIOR.— Mr. Henry Senior, sand merchant, of Sand House, Balby Road, died on Sunday last, at the ripe old age of 74. He was out on the Thursday, but was taken ill the same day with a very bad attack of bronchitis, to which he was somewhat predisposed, and pneumonia supervened. The property on which the deceased has lived for many years, and on which he died, was inherited by him from his father, Mr. William Senior, who was in his time the only sand merchant in the district. As a young man, the deceased was employed in some capacity or other upon the navigation at Barnsley, but on his father's death returned to Doncaster to carry on the sand business. At that time the property was surrounded by open fields. Deceased built the Alma Inn and lived there for some time, and played an important part in the development of the Victoria Street neighbourhood. It was during the earlier part of his ownership of the sand-pit, that the idea of cutting a house out of a rather hard portion met with in the strata which he was working took shape in his mind

Fig. 6.31 Extract from Henry Senior's obituary, April 1900.

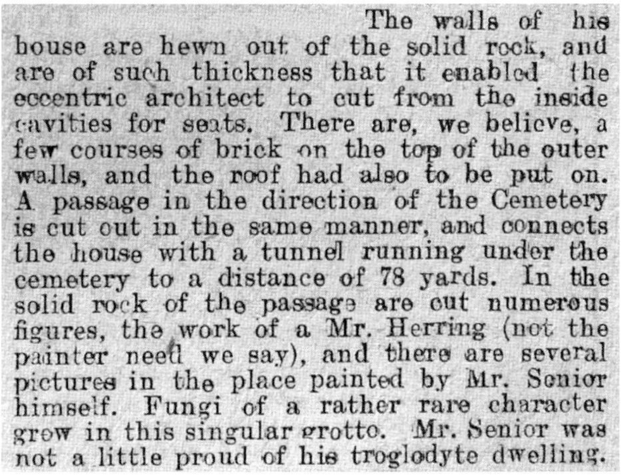

The walls of his house are hewn out of the solid rock, and are of such thickness that it enabled the eccentric architect to cut from the inside cavities for seats. There are, we believe, a few courses of brick on the top of the outer walls, and the roof had also to be put on. A passage in the direction of the Cemetery is cut out in the same manner, and connects the house with a tunnel running under the cemetery to a distance of 78 yards. In the solid rock of the passage are cut numerous figures, the work of a Mr. Herring (not the painter need we say), and there are several pictures in the place painted by Mr. Senior himself. Fungi of a rather rare character grow in this singular grotto. Mr. Senior was not a little proud of his troglodyte dwelling.

But there is another section of this newspaper article which demonstrates remarkable foresight. In referring to the Sand House, Henry Senior's obituarist recorded:

> ... it is in association with that unique dwelling and its passages that the name of Mr. Henry Senior will go down in posterity, if that honour should befall him, for the changes of time in such a rapidly developing neighbourhood may clear the whole thing away.

Epilogue
And Finally
... or Perhaps Not?

Fig. E1 Ann Bell in the tunnel entrance from the former summer-house.

AND FINALLY... OR PERHAPS NOT?

Back in my childhood days, when my family used to talk about the mysterious subject of the Sand House, little did I realise how important it would become to me in later life. Even in those early days of research almost thirty years ago, the idea of two books and well over 100 illustrated talks would have seemed completely ridiculous. So what was the turning point? As I look back now, I realise what a major influence my 1984 visit to the Catacombs and Cloisters had upon me. If seeing the photograph of the Elephant and Mahout on the cover of this book had an impact on you, the reader, imagine how I felt when my torch beam fell upon the carving itself and I viewed it with my own eyes. My spine still tingles a little as I recall that February afternoon and I realise the inspiration that it provided.

Some of my memories of that underground visit are vivid, while others have faded with time. I remember the keen sense of anticipation as I and my fellow 'explorers' – including my wife, Ann – were briefed, not only about the safety arrangements that would be employed, but also about the historical background to the tunnels, much of which I was already familiar with. Once we had travelled from Doncaster Council's offices, where the briefing was held, to the site itself, we were given a final reminder about the safety precautions and what to do if the air monitoring equipment's alarm sounded, before being split into two groups. First one group would enter the tunnels, under supervision, and the second group would have to wait until they were safely back on the surface before taking their own turn. While Ann and I waited on the surface, I started taking some photographs, reminding myself to take as many shots as I could when down below, as this was a once-in-a-lifetime opportunity.

Eventually our turn came to descend the ladder that had been secured within the 2.5 m square temporary access shaft close to Silverwood House. At the foot of the ladder I stepped onto a sandy slope, which I followed downwards for several metres before the floor levelled out and I found myself at the northern end of the Cloisters, near to the Catacombs.

Clearly, the main purpose of there being a temporary access into the tunnels was to facilitate the proposed infilling of the remaining voids and not to provide tourism opportunities for interested relatives of the tunnels' creators. While the contractor's staff, who were supervising the visit, were courteous and helpful, they were not about to let us wander off on our own. I quickly gained the impression that my fellow visitors and I should treat this experience as a significant concession afforded to us by our hosts and be grateful for it ... which I was!

Once I had found my bearings, I looked closely at the sandstone walls and roof and quickly spotted the carving of the Cherub. But instead of seeing the Cherub looking down on me from above head height, as in the early picture postcard that I had seen, it had been buried up to forehead level by the earlier partial infilling of the Catacombs. Nevertheless, what a thrill it was to see the first of those carvings, which I had only seen on photographs previously. The detail that I could see, such as the Cherub's hair, was remarkable. This really was already proving to be quite an experience. I just had time to take a couple of photographs looking northwards into the Catacombs before being urged onwards towards the Cloisters, where the other members of my group had headed.

The next obstacle which Ann and I had to negotiate was what is often referred to as the 'ten-foot drop'. This is where a masonry wall had been built across the Cloisters in the 1930s, between the Elephant and the Clown carvings, and it was retaining compacted sand on its north side right up to the top of the wall, this being the same fill that partially obscured the Cherub. A short ladder had been placed against the wall, which was actually nearer 2 m than 3 m high, and we climbed down to what must have been more or less the original floor level of the Cloisters.

As I descended the short ladder at the 'ten-foot drop' I realised that the carved Elephant stood to my left and then, stepping back from the foot of the ladder, I noticed the Clown to my right. I think it was at this point that I suddenly realised the significance of what I was doing and seeing. My great-great-grandfather *had actually walked along this tunnel* on innumerable occasions: he may even have had a direct hand in producing some of the carvings I was seeing. These carvings had been created over a century earlier and it was entirely possible, indeed, likely that I was now to be one of the last people to see them before they were entombed in a pulverised fuel ash 'plaster-cast'.

The only light in the tunnels came from torches that I and my fellow explorers were carrying and from the occasional split-second flashlight of cameras. This was proving to be quite a handicap, because to take a photograph of a particular feature one first had to aim the camera in the right direction, which was proving none too easy. These were the pre-digital days, so there were no second chances. If I didn't obtain a good set of photographs now, then I never would.

With each step I seemed to find a new subject to study. Although this was reality, I had to remind myself that I hadn't suddenly been transported into a H. Rider Haggard novel or an Indiana Jones movie!

Ann and I wandered on a little further along the Cloisters, or at least as far as our group's supervisors would permit us, which didn't seem terribly far. In practice, it was just far enough to see the bust of the King and those of the Queens Elizabeth I and Victoria in the seventh adit, taking photographs all the while. Beyond that point was darkness: one of the contractor's staff told me that the tunnel was blocked a few metres further along by the infill, which supported the dual carriageway above. So there was nowhere further to go in that direction and, reluctantly, I turned to head back towards the access point, conscious of an unspoken urgency to end the visit.

A few more photographs were fitted in as Ann and I waited our turns to climb the 'ten-foot drop' and then it was back up the sandy slope, which I later realised had once been the location of the steps up to the back of the summer house in the Sand House garden. And almost before I knew it, Ann and I were back above ground and my one-and-only chance to visit this unique place had ended.

What mixed emotions I felt as, on the one hand, I was so elated by what I had seen but, on the other, I knew that it was about to be destroyed, or at least made completely inaccessible. I didn't know at that time about the books and illustrated talks that would eventually serve as a record of Henry Senior's marvellous creation, but as I stood alongside Silverwood House in the gathering gloom of a late-February afternoon, I did know that there was a story there that needed to be told.

It was not until many years later that I realised that I didn't possess a single photograph of myself inside the Sand House tunnels! However, I had taken a few photographs that showed Ann down there and one of them is reproduced here (Fig. E1). It also serves as a small 'thank you', which may go a little way towards compensating Ann for the numerous hours of my time that she has had to forfeit when the lure of the Sand House proved too great.

So what of the future? Some may say that the story of the Sand House ended when the last cubic metre of pulverised fuel ash was pumped into the tunnels in 1984, but I believe that it still lives on. At the very least, snippets of information will continue to be discovered, as they have been over the past twenty-six years. And who knows, when the St James' Street area is eventually re-developed once again, the opportunity may be taken in the twenty-first century to uncover the remains of the Sand House and to afford this fascinating and unique creation the acknowledgement and respect so sadly denied to it by our forebears in the twentieth century. I just hope that I'm still around to witness it!

Richard Bell, 2010

LIST OF FIGURES, NEWSPAPER REFERENCES
AND REFERENCE SOURCES

Front Cover   Photograph of 'Elephant and Mahout', Cloisters, Sand House, Doncaster
               (hand-coloured by Edwin Dixon).

Page 2   Top – Sand House front garden, looking north.
               Bottom – Long Room interior *c.* 1912.

Page 4   The Cloisters facing south.

Page 6   Front garden in snow.

Chapter 1 – William Senior and the Sand Pit
Fig. 1.1   The Great Fungus in the 'sewerage tunnel.'
Fig. 1.2   Artist's impression of Senior's sand pit *c.* 1830s.
Fig. 1.3   Plan showing land ownership *c.* 1820 – *c.* 1870.
Fig. 1.4   Route of main drain constructed *c.* 1854.
Fig. 1.5   Senior's sand pit with line of main drain.
Fig. 1.6   Longitudinal section from St Sepulchre Gate to the Carr.
Fig. 1.7   Artist's impression indicating position of Catacombs.
Fig. 1.8   Advertisement for sale of freehold building ground, January 1856.
Fig. 1.9   Advertisement for sale of houses and building ground, May 1856.
Fig. 1.10   Artist's impression of the original four-roomed Sand House.
Fig. 1.11   The Great Fungus in the 'sewerage tunnel.'
Fig. 1.12   Public Notice from William Senior.
Fig. 1.13   Notice of William Senior's death.

Chapter 2 – Henry Senior and the Sand House
Fig. 2.1   Statue of 'Summer.'
Fig. 2.2   Sand House gable.
Fig. 2.3   Artist's impression of the completed Sand House *c.* 1880.

Fig. 2.4   Lower floor room layout with thumbnails.
Fig. 2.5   Upper floor room layout with thumbnails.
Fig. 2.6   The Long Room, pre-1900.
Fig. 2.7   Recessed chair to the left of the Long Room fireplace.
Fig. 2.8   Fireplace and recessed chairs in Long Room.
Fig. 2.9   Statue of 'Summer.'
Fig. 2.10   Carving on office corner.
Fig. 2.11   Back of Sand House.
Fig. 2.12   Panoramic view of Sand House area from Green Dyke Lane, *c.* 1900.
Fig. 2.13   Stable door and carvings of Henry and Mary Senior.
Fig. 2.14   Front garden looking north towards Long Room.
Fig. 2.15   Figure, allegedly Henry Senior, seated in garden; gable to the left.
Fig. 2.16   Mary Senior *c.* 1880.
Fig. 2.17   'Rumour of ghost' newspaper article, 29 June 1883.
Fig. 2.18   Figures seated outside the Long Room.
Fig. 2.19   Figures seated in the front garden.
Fig. 2.20   Handbill advertising Don Castle.
Fig. 2.21   Sand House, tunnels and surrounding area *c.* 1900.
Fig. 2.22   Public notice from Henry Senior, 23 July 1897.
Fig. 2.23   Henry Senior's funeral card.
Fig. 2.24   The Senior family vault in Hyde Park Cemetery, Doncaster.

Chapter 3 – The Tunnels and Carvings

Fig. 3.1   'Pat' the Irishman.
Fig. 3.2   Cross section through the Cloisters, looking south.
Fig. 3.3   Plan of Cloisters, illustrating major carvings with thumbnails.
Fig. 3.4   The Cloisters, looking south.
Fig. 3.5   The Cherub.
Fig. 3.6   'Molly' or 'Biddy' the Irishwoman.
Fig. 3.7   'Pat' the Irishman.
Fig. 3.8   The Clown.
Fig. 3.9   The Elephant and Mahout.
Fig. 3.10   Pope and frieze beneath.
Fig. 3.11   Floral boss.
Fig. 3.12   King.
Fig. 3.13   Queen Victoria in maturity.
Fig. 3.14   The Cloisters, looking north.
Fig. 3.15   Queen Victoria in her youth.
Fig. 3.16   Seat thought to have links with St George's Church.
Fig. 3.17   The Cloisters, looking south.

Chapter 4 – The Sand House In Corporation Ownership

Fig. 4.1   Possibly the last photograph taken of the Sand House.
Fig. 4.2   The Sand House seen from Green Dyke Lane *c.* 1912.

Fig. 4.3   Hague family *c.* 1918.
Fig. 4.4   The Long Room *c.* 1920.
Fig. 4.5   William James Green, photographer.
Fig. 4.6   Shikell employee and horse with Victoria Street in background.
Fig. 4.7   Arthur Shikell posing at rear of Sand House.
Fig. 4.8   Shikell horsemen and horses: St Sepulchre Gate in distance.
Fig. 4.9   Sand House front elevation with Victoria Street above.
Fig. 4.10   Wheatley Senior School girls inspect the Sand House, 30 July 1936.
Fig. 4.11   Aerial view taken in June 1951.
Fig. 4.12   Subsidence damage to Victoria Street house, 20 August 1953.

Chapter 5 – The Hemingways and No. 69 Victoria Street

Fig. 5.1   Portrait of William Hemingway, *c.* 1915.
Fig. 5.2   Blank invoice.
Fig. 5.3   William Hemingway, August 1900.
Fig. 5.4   Steps entering cavern from cellar of No. 69 Victoria Street.
Fig. 5.5   Carving in cavern below No. 69 Victoria Street.
Fig. 5.6   Carving in cavern below No. 69 Victoria Street.
Fig. 5.7   Carving in cavern below No. 69 Victoria Street.
Fig. 5.8   Carving in cavern below No. 69 Victoria Street.
Fig. 5.9   No. 69 Victoria Street, December 1967.
Fig. 5.10   Partially infilled cavern below No. 69 Victoria Street.
Fig. 5.11   Extent and location of cavern beneath No. 69 Victoria Street.

Chapter 6 – Echoes From the Past

Fig. 6.1   Jeff. Hoggarth seen in the Cloisters, January 1976.
Fig. 6.2   Sand House site from Green Dyke Lane, June 1961.
Fig. 6.3   Section of Sand House site with Albert and Elsworth Streets beyond.
Fig. 6.4   Excavation for tunnel survey, May 1964.
Fig. 6.5   The Catacombs.
Fig. 6.6   Manhole under Green Dyke Lane.
Fig. 6.7   'Sewerage tunnel' below Hyde Park (Doncaster) Cemetery.
Fig. 6.8   Typical foundations for large structures in poor ground.
Fig. 6.9   Borehole sunk in Green Dyke Lane, 1976.
Fig. 6.10   Jeff. Hoggarth descending into the Cloisters, 1976.
Fig. 6.11   A decorated adit in the Cloisters.
Fig. 6.12   John Little in the Cloisters, January 1976.
Fig. 6.13   Jeff. Hoggarth examining the Clown.
Fig. 6.14   Stephen McClarence in the Cloisters.
Fig. 6.15   Cloisters carvings in January 1976.
Fig. 6.16   Cloisters carvings in January 1976.
Fig. 6.17   Cloisters carving in January 1976.
Fig. 6.18   Present street layout showing Sand House site with thumbnails.
Fig. 6.19   Shaft access into Catacombs and Cloisters, February 1984.

Fig. 6.20   An employee of G. L. Quine with safety equipment in the Cloisters.
Fig. 6.21   Remains of the Elephant and Mahout, February 1984.
Fig. 6.22   The poor state of the Clown, February 1984.
Fig. 6.23   The King still in good condition, February 1984.
Fig. 6.24   Backfilled boreholes to rear of Cadeby House.
Fig. 6.25   Plan showing when various sections of the tunnels were infilled.
Fig. 6.26   Hyde Park (Doncaster) Cemetery over line of remaining tunnel.
Fig. 6.27   Looking southwards on the former line of Victoria Street, July 2010.
Fig. 6.28   Looking northwards over the Sand House site, July 2010.
Fig. 6.29   The Sand House superimposed on the present-day landscape.
Fig. 6.30   Extract from Henry Senior's obituary, April 1900.
Fig. 6.31   Extract from Henry Senior's obituary, April 1900.

Epilogue – And Finally… Or Perhaps Not
Fig. E1   Ann Bell in the tunnel entrance from the former summer-house.

Back Cover   Figures seated in the front garden.

LIST OF NEWSPAPER REFERENCES

D. N. L. Gaz.	19/1/1838	Employee of W. Senior charged with stealing.
D. N. L. Gaz.	8/11/1844	Employee of W. Senior killed in accident at work.
D. N. L. Gaz.	4/5/1849	'Bail Court, Tuesday, May 1.'
D. N. L. Gaz.	13/5/1853	'Doncaster Board of Health.'
D. N. L. Gaz.	29/7/1853	'The sand pit outfall drain and the rock sand tunnel.'
D. N. L. Gaz.	9/9/1853	'Rock sand tunnel.'
D. N. L. Gaz.	9/9/1853	'The rock sand tunnel.'
D. N. L. Gaz.	11/1/1856	Advertisement for property sale by Mr Senior.
D. N. L. Gaz.	2/5/1856	Advertisement for property sale by Mr Senior.
D. N. L. Gaz.	1/5/1857	Alleged assault by W. Senior.
D. N. L. Gaz.	16/4/1858	'Enormous fungus – interesting to naturalists.'
I. L. N.	15/5/1858	'Great fungus in tunnel.'
D. N. L. Gaz.	3/6/1859	Public notice.
D. N. L. Gaz.	17/6/1859	Advertisement for sale of Thief Lane Close.
D. N. L. Gaz.	24/6/1859	Report on sale of Thief Lane Close.
D. N. L. Gaz.	8/7/1859	Death of W. Senior
D. N. L. Gaz.	29/12/1865	'A house unfit for human habitation.'
Don. Gaz.	22/6/1883	'An alleged ghost at Doncaster.'

Don. Gaz.	29/6/1883	'The rumour of a ghost at the Sand House.'
Don. Gaz.	13/2/1885	Advertisement for sale of Don Castle Brewery.
Don. Gaz.	14/3/1890	Advertisement for property sale by H. Senior.
Don. Review	8/1894	'The sand rock house at Doncaster.'
Don. Gaz.	23/4/1897	Advertisement for 'Don Castle Pleasure Ground'.
Don. Gaz.	23/7/1897	Public notice after H. Senior's 'misfortune'.
Don. Gaz.	13/8/1897	'Jubilee Celebrations.'
Don. Gaz.	6/4/1900	'Death of Mr. H. Senior.'
Don. Gaz.	13/4/1900	Public notice.
Don. Chron.	15/6/1900	Advertisement for sale of Sand House.
Don. Gaz.	22/6/1900	Advertisement for sale of Sand House.
Don. Gaz.	2/8/1912	'Subterranean Doncaster.'
Don. Gaz.	22/8/1919	'A unique Doncaster housing scheme.'
Don. Gaz.	21/7/1932	Death of Thomas Hague.
Don. Gaz.	28/7/1932	Applications invited for post of foreman.
Don. Gaz.	16/3/1933	'Quaint old names.'
Don. Gaz.	10/8/1933	'"Sandy" Senior's mammoth fungus.'
Don. Gaz.	3/1/1935	'The Sand House.'
Don. Gaz.	c.1936	'Sand House history.'
Don. Gaz.	c.1936	'Dancing nights at Sand House.'
Don. Gaz.	11/6/1936	'From church to Sand House.'
Don. Gaz.	30/7/1936	'Local curiosity.'
Don. Chron.	18/12/1952	Letter to the editor.
Don. Chron.	18/12/1952	'The Sand House.'
Don. Chron.	24/12/1952	'The Sand House.'
Don. Chron.	1/1/1953	'Memories of the unique Sand House.'
Don. Chron.	20/8/1953	'Subsidence threat to street.'
Don. Chron.	20/8/1953	'Sand House recalled.'
Don. Gaz.	29/6/1961	'Castle of sand was in quarry.'
Don. Chron.	21/12/1961	'Probe may start for buried castle.'
Don. Gaz.	25/4/1963	'Skyscrapers over castle of sand?'
Don. Chron.	25/4/1963	'Old tunnels problem for today's planners.'
Don. Gaz.	2/5/1963	'I remember visiting the famous Sand House quarry.'
Yorks. E. Post	4/12/1963	'The sand house that George [*sic*] built.'
Yorks. E. Post	9/12/1963	'He lived in the house of sand.'
Yorks. E. Post	17/12/1963	'Tunnel memory recalled.'
Don. Gaz. & Chron.	7/5/1964	'Digging out the house that "Sandy" built.'
Yorks. E. Post	8/5/1964	'Sand House re-discovered.'
Don. Gaz. & Chron.	14/5/1964	'That house of sand.'
Don. Gaz. & Chron.	4/6/1964	'Business to make way for progress.'
Don. Gaz. & Chron.	4/6/1964	'Sandy's house.'

Don. Gaz. & Chron.	11/6/1964	'"Sandy's" descendant.'
Don. E. Post	21/12/1967	'Like a waxworks but all in stone.'
Unidentified	c. 1967	'Sandstone carvings may now be buried for ever.'
Don. E. Post	11/1/1968	'Museum fail to save carvings.'
Don. E. Post	16/1/1968	'Sand entombs cavern's secrets.'
Don. Gaz.	18/1/1968	'Balby subsidence fears are calmed.'
Don. Gaz.	18/1/1968	'Nostalgia and warning note.'
Don. E. Post	20/4/1968	'Mystery of the 'lost street' may never be solved.'
Unidentified	c. 1969	'Bid to unearth carvings fails.'
Don. E. Post	22/1/1976	'Engineers probe the Sand House.'
Don. E. Post	27/1/1976	'Memories of the Sand House.'
Don. E. Post	28/1/1976	'E. P. throws light on the past.'
Don. E. Post	31/1/1976	'Son of Sandy (junior).'
Don. E. Post	5/2/1976	'Lived at the Sand House.'
Fib. Post	19/3/1976	'John's ancestors lived in house made of sand.'
Sun. Tel.	28/3/1976	'Road men uncover Victorian eccentric's carved wonderland.'
Daily Tel.?	29/3/1976?	'No tears shed over lost cave carvings.'
Ch. Surv.	7/1976	Doncaster sand tunnels.
Unidentified	c. 1976	'Don Castle.'
Unidentified	c. 1976	'Tunnel art halts work on road.'
Unidentified	c. 1976	'Underground art show.'
Weekend	2/2/1977	'End of the road for a fantasy.'
Don. Free Press	Jan.-Mar. 1978	'Do you remember?'
Don. Free Press	1/6/1978	'Resident recalls a unique building.'
Don. Free Press	1/5/1980	'Sand House.'
Don. Free Press	8/5/1980	'Sand House (continued).'
Don. E. Post	17/2/1982	'Discovery in town sewer collapse.'
Don. E. Post	8/4/1983	'Echoes from the past.'
Don. Star	?/6/1983	'Sewer collapse near Balby homes.'
Don. Star	13/12/1983	'Last look at Doncaster's old sand 'castle'.'
Don. Star	19/12/1983	'Old sand grotto to be sealed.'
Don. Star	23/1/1984	'Secrets of Don Castle.'
Don. Star	20/2/1984	'Bid to save folly.'
Don. Star	21/2/1984	'Last look at Sandy's masterpiece.'
Don. Star	20/11/1986	'Secrets in the sand.'
Don. Ad.	2/4/1987	'The Sand House.'
Thorne Ad.	4/1987	'The Sand House.'
Don. Star	29/12/1987	'Veteran of Sand House dies at 90.'
Don. Star	14/7/1988	'Treasure buried for ever.'
Don. Free Press	28/7/1988	'Sand cave story told.'

Don. Star	28/7/1988	'Lurid tales among the Doncaster gangsters.'
Don. Star	7/9/1988	'The dark secret of 69 Victoria Street.'
Yorks. Post	27/10/1990	'Digging up the sands of regret.'
Don. Star	24/6/1993	'The world underground.'
Ent. Scene	16/12/1993	'Walls nine feet thick!'
Ent. Scene	23/12/1993	'Lost memorial to a lifetime's work is beneath Balby.'
Ent. Scene	3/2/1994	'Memories of the amazing Sand House.'
Past Times	4/5/2000	Making a house from sandstone.'
Ax. Her.	10/11/2000	'Captivating Sand House talk for society.'
Times Then	12/2000	'Tunnelling back through history.'
Don. Star	24/7/2003	'Stupidity' left a void in Doncaster's heritage
Don. Free Press	11/2/2010	'Sand House stars in first heritage festival.'

Key to names of publications

Ax. Her.	Axholme Herald
Ch. Surv.	Chartered Surveyor magazine
Daily Tel.	Daily Telegraph
D. N. L. Gaz.	Doncaster, Nottingham and Lincoln Gazette
Don. Ad.	Doncaster Advertiser
Don. Chron.	Doncaster Chronicle
Don. E. Post	Doncaster Evening Post
Don. Free Press	Doncaster Free Press
Don. Gaz.	Doncaster Gazette
Don. Gaz. & Chron.	Doncaster Gazette and Chronicle
Don. Review	The Doncaster Review
Don. Star	Doncaster Star
Ent. Scene	The Entertainment Scene
Fib. Post	Fibres Post (in-house newspaper of ICI Fibres)
I. L. N.	Illustrated London News
Past Times	Past Times (a local history publication in Doncaster)
Sun. Tel.	Sunday Telegraph
Thorne Ad.	Thorne Advertiser
Times Then	Times Then and Now (a local history newspaper in Doncaster)
Weekend	Weekend Magazine
Yorks. E. Post	Yorkshire Evening Post
Yorks. Post	Yorkshire Post

REFERENCE SOURCES

Baines, E. (1822) *History, Directory and Gazetteer of the County of York*. Vol. 1. West Riding. Leeds.
Doncaster Gazette Directories (1912, 1913).

Hatfield, C. W. (1866-70) *Historical Notices of Doncaster.* Vols. 1-3. Doncaster.

Kelly, E. R. (1861, 1877) *The Post Office Directory of the West Riding of Yorkshire.* London.

Slater, I. (1848, 1858) *Directory of Northern England.* Manchester.

White, W. (1837) *History, Gazetteer and Directory of the West Riding of Yorkshire.* Vols. 1-2. Sheffield.

White, W. (1867) *Directory of the East Riding of Yorkshire.* Sheffield.

Wormald, H. R. (1974) *Modern Doncaster, Progress and Development 1836-1974.*

* * * * *

Census Returns, 1841, 1851, 1861, 1871, 1881 (Barnsley Library Service; Derbyshire County Library Headquarters, Matlock; D. M. B. C. Library Services; National Archives, London).

Certificates of Births, Deaths and Marriages (General Register Office, London).

Deeds of Land Ownership (Registry of Deeds, West Yorkshire County Record Office, Wakefield).

Doncaster Cemetery Records (Doncaster Archives).

Doncaster Corporation Minutes (D. M. B. C. Library Services).

Drawings: HGE/0450/1, Investigation into carriageway collapse, St James' Street, Doncaster; HGE/0513/2, St James' Street sand galleries; HGE/0513/4, St James' Street sand galleries, services location plan (D. M. B. C. Design Services Directorate).

Local Board of Health Minutes (D. M. B. C. Library Services).

Newspapers (British Library Newspaper Library, Colindale; D. M. B. C. Library Services).

Notebooks of R. E. Ford, Borough Surveyor 1916-1947 (D. M. B. C. Library Services)

Ordnance Survey Maps; 60 ins scale, 1852 (surveyed 1850); 6 ins scale, 1854 (surveyed 1849-50); 25 ins scale, 1892 (surveyed 1890); 25 ins scale, 1903 (surveyed 1888-90, revised 1901); 50 ins scale, 1930 (surveyed 1928-29).

Parish Registers (Derbyshire County Record Office, Matlock; D. M. B. C. Library Services; West Yorkshire County Record Office, Wakefield).

Register of Beer and Spirit Licences (D. M. B. C. Library Services).

Technical Report No. 1318, Geotechnical and Concrete Services Ltd, Sheffield 3/6/1964 (D. M. B. C. Design Services Directorate).

War Office Records (National Archives, London).